Samuel French Acting Edition

The White Sheep of the Family

by L. du Garde Peach
and Ian Hay

SAMUELFRENCH.COM   SAMUELFRENCH.CO.UK

Copyright © 1953 by Samuel French, Ltd.
All Rights Reserved

THE WHITE SHEEP OF THE FAMILY is fully protected under the copyright laws of the United States of America, the British Commonwealth, including Canada, and all other countries of the Copyright Union. All rights, including professional and amateur stage productions, recitation, lecturing, public reading, motion picture, radio broadcasting, television and the rights of translation into foreign languages are strictly reserved.

ISBN 978-0-573-61785-0

www.SamuelFrench.com
www.SamuelFrench.co.uk

For Production Enquiries

United States and Canada
Info@SamuelFrench.com
1-866-598-8449

United Kingdom and Europe
Plays@SamuelFrench.co.uk
020-7255-4302

Each title is subject to availability from Samuel French, depending upon country of performance. Please be aware that *THE WHITE SHEEP OF THE FAMILY* may not be licensed by Samuel French in your territory. Professional and amateur producers should contact the nearest Samuel French office or licensing partner to verify availability.

CAUTION: Professional and amateur producers are hereby warned that *THE WHITE SHEEP OF THE FAMILY* is subject to a licensing fee. Publication of this play(s) does not imply availability for performance. Both amateurs and professionals considering a production are strongly advised to apply to Samuel French before starting rehearsals, advertising, or booking a theatre. A licensing fee must be paid whether the title(s) is presented for charity or gain and whether or not admission is charged. Professional/Stock licensing fees are quoted upon application to Samuel French.

No one shall make any changes in this title(s) for the purpose of production. No part of this book may be reproduced, stored in a retrieval system, or transmitted in any form, by any means, now known or yet to be invented, including mechanical, electronic, photocopying, recording, videotaping, or otherwise, without the prior written permission of the publisher. No one shall upload this title(s), or part of this title(s), to any social media websites.

For all enquiries regarding motion picture, television, and other media rights, please contact Samuel French.

MUSIC USE NOTE

Licensees are solely responsible for obtaining formal written permission from copyright owners to use copyrighted music in the performance of this play and are strongly cautioned to do so. If no such permission is obtained by the licensee, then the licensee must use only original music that the licensee owns and controls. Licensees are solely responsible and liable for all music clearances and shall indemnify the copyright owners of the play(s) and their licensing agent, Samuel French, against any costs, expenses, losses and liabilities arising from the use of music by licensees. Please contact the appropriate music licensing authority in your territory for the rights to any incidental music.

IMPORTANT BILLING AND CREDIT REQUIREMENTS

If you have obtained performance rights to this title, please refer to your licensing agreement for important billing and credit requirements.

THE WHITE SHEEP OF THE FAMILY

Presented at the Piccadilly Theatre, London, W.1, on 11th October, 1951, with the following cast of characters—

(*In the order of their appearance*)

ALICE WINTER .... *Joyce Carey*
JANET, the maid.................... *Brenda Bancroft*
JAMES WINTER, J.P.................... *Jack Hulbert*
PAT WINTER, his daughter............ *Sonia Williams*
ASSISTANT COMMISSIONER JOHN PRESTON,
  Campbell Copelin
THE VICAR .... *Denys Blakelock*
SAM JACKSON.................... *Cyril Chamberlain*
PETER WINTER, James's son .... *Derek Blomfield*
ANGELA PRESTON, Peter's fiancée .... *Rona Anderson*

SYNOPSIS OF SCENES

The action of the play passes in the living-room of the Winters' house in Hampstead.

ACT ONE
An evening in August.

ACT TWO
SCENE 1—*The following morning.*
SCENE 2—*The evening of the same day.*

ACT THREE
The following morning.

TIME: *The present.*

The White Sheep of the Family

ACT ONE

SCENE: *The living-room of the Winters' house in Hampstead. An evening in August. The room is a pleasant one and is comfortably furnished. There are wide folding windows Up Right opening on to a large terrace with a view of the garden beyond. A door Up Center gives access to other parts of the house and a door Up Left leads to* JAMES WINTER'S *office. The fireplace is Left, and there is a small window Down Right overlooking the garden. There is a set of bookshelves Left of the door Up Center, so constructed that the right section can be opened outwards to reveal a cupboard behind it. A portrait of an elderly Victorian gentleman hangs over the mantelpiece. This picture is hinged and can be swung outwards to reveal a cupboard behind it. Below the window Up Right, there is a panel low down in the wall concealing a practical safe with a combination lock. There are armchairs, Right Center, Left Center and Down Left. A large comfortable sofa stands Center. There is a cabinet for drinks Down Right, a desk and telephone Right and small tables Right Center and Center. (See the Ground Plan and Photograph of the Scene.)*

When the CURTAIN *rises, the lights are on, but the window curtains are not yet closed.* MRS. ALICE WINTER *is seated on the sofa, engaged in sewing cushion covers. She is a charming woman aged about fifty.* JANET, *a trim and attractive housemaid, is standing at the window Up Right. She closes the window curtains, moves to the window Down Right, draws the curtain across it, then stands below the table Right Center.*

JANET. Shall I serve coffee, madam?

ALICE. Has Mr. Winter come in yet?

JANET. I haven't heard him.

ALICE. I don't suppose he'll be long. We'll have it as soon as he comes.

JANET. Very good, madam.

ALICE. Bring the spirit lamp, Janet. After dining at the club, Mr. Winter likes his coffee hot. For a change, I suppose.

JANET. Don't they serve it hot in clubs, madam?

ALICE. Apparently not. I suppose it might keep the members awake. Mr. Winter's a member of three clubs and he says the coffee in each is worse than the other two. What's the time, Janet?

JANET. Just on nine.

ALICE. When you've brought the coffee, suppose you go out for an hour. It's a nice evening.

JANET. I might be in time for the big picture at the *Scala*. It's a crime film.

ALICE. Morbid girl. Do you really like crime films?

JANET. I like a good laugh.

(JAMES WINTER *enters Up Center. He carries copies of the "Evening News," the "Evening Standard," and the "Star."*)

JAMES. (*Moving below the sofa.*) Good evening, my dear. Good evening, Janet. (*He kisses* ALICE.) Evening papers? (*He hands her the "Evening News" and the "Star."*)

ALICE. My dear James, why do men buy so many evening papers?

JAMES. (*Crossing to the fireplace.*) To take the edge off tomorrow's depressing news.

ACT I WHITE SHEEP OF THE FAMILY

ALICE. You're home early. Did you have a nice dinner? (*She puts the papers on the table Center.*)

JAMES. I was dining at the club.

ALICE. Of course. I'm sorry.

JAMES. I don't know why I belong to the *Athenaeum*.

ALICE. The outside's full of charm.

JAMES. The inside's full of bishops.

ALICE. Don't you like bishops, dear?

JAMES. Oh, charming! But the higher clergy dine so early that there's nothing left but loaves and fishes for the poor starving laity. How about some coffee, Janet?

JANET. I'll get it now, sir.

ALICE. As quick as you can, Janet. Then you'll be in good time for your crime film.

JAMES. Mind you don't get led astray, Janet. What's it called?

JANET. *Crime Pays No Dividends*, sir.

JAMES. The government will be delighted.

ALICE. It must grieve the Income Tax people not to be able to assess a burglar.

JAMES. Oh, they'd never do a thing like that, darling. Breach of etiquette. (*He crosses to* JANET.) Honor among thieves and all that. (*He takes a coin from his pocket and hands it to* JANET.) For the furtherance of crime.

JANET. Oooh, thanks ever so, Mr. Winter, sir. (*She moves to the door Up Center.*) I'll tell you all about it when I come back.

JAMES. (*Perching himself on the right arm of the sofa.*) Remind me to keep out of her way.

(PAT WINTER *enters Up Center.*)

JANET. (*To* PAT.) I'm going to see *Crime Pays No Dividends*.

PAT. You're lucky. I'm going to the Opera.

(*The front doorbell rings.*)

ALICE. Isn't that the bell, Janet?

JANET. Yes, madam. (JANET *exits Up Center.*)

JAMES. (*To* PAT.) You're looking very charming tonight, my dear.

PAT. (*Moving to Right of the sofa.*) Thank you, darling. (*She puts her wrap and handbag on the stool above the sofa.*)

JAMES. Is it quite fair to *Covent Garden?* All eyes will be on you.

PAT. I should hate that. (*She crosses to the fireplace.*)

ALICE. Are you expecting anybody, James?

JAMES. It might be Sam Jackson.

PAT. (*With a little grimace.*) All diamonds and Brylcreem.

ALICE. He probably has a heart of gold, dear.

JAMES. I would suggest a baser metal.

(JANET *enters Up Center. She carries a visiting card.*)

JANET. (*Moving to Right of* JAMES.) A gentleman to see you, sir. (*She hands the card to him.*)

ALICE. (*Correcting her kindly.*) On a salver, Janet. That's the right way to do it.

JANET. Thank you, madam. I'll remember.

JAMES. (*Reading the card.*) "Assistant Commissioner John Preston, Scotland Yard."

(JANET *gives a little exclamation.*)

ALICE. What's the matter, Janet? You look quite frightened.

JAMES. (*Smiling.*) Too many crime films, eh? Don't worry, Janet, he hasn't called professionally. (*He rises.*) Show the Commissioner in.

JANET. Yes, sir. (JANET *exits Up Center.*)

PAT. (*Moving Down Left.*) Assistant Commissioner, Scotland Yard. He sounds very grand.

ALICE. Do you know him, dear?

JAMES. (*Crossing to the fireplace.*) Yes, in my capacity

ACT I   WHITE SHEEP OF THE FAMILY   9

as a magistrate. A nice type; an old soldier, I fancy.
(*He puts the newspaper on the table Center.*)
PAT. What does he want?

(JANET *enters Up Center and stands Right of the open
door.*)

JANET. (*Announcing; a little apprehensively.*) The
Commissionaire, sir.

(ASSISTANT COMMISSIONER JOHN PRESTON *enters Up
Center. He is a pleasant ex-military officer aged
about fifty. He gives* JANET *a little glance of amusement.* JAMES *moves below the armchair Left Center.*
ALICE *rises.* JANET *exits Up Center.*)

PRESTON. (*Crossing to* JAMES.) Good evening, Winter.
JAMES. Good evening, Commissioner. Nice to see you
again. (*To* ALICE.) My dear, Assistant Commissioner
Preston.
ALICE. (*Pleasantly.*) How do you do?
PRESTON. (*Shaking hands with* ALICE.) How do you
do, Mrs. Winter?
JAMES. And my daughter, Pat.
PRESTON. (*Crossing to* PAT *and shaking hands with
her.*) How do you do?
PAT. How do you do?
PRESTON. I have a daughter almost your age. Are you
the only member of the family?
PAT. No. There's a brother.
ALICE. (*Rather hastily.*) He is staying with friends at
present. Do sit down, won't you?
PRESTON. Thank you. (*He sits on the sofa at the Left
end.*) Your little maid—wasn't that the girl the Vicar
brought to your notice?

(ALICE *sits on the sofa at the Right end.*)

JAMES. Yes—you put her father away, you remember?

PRESTON. (*Smiling.*) He is still with us. How is the girl doing?

ALICE. Very well—she's a very nice girl, in fact.

PRESTON. It was good of you to take her.

ALICE. I can assure you, in these days a girl like Janet is a godsend.

(JANET *enters Up Center. She carries a tray of coffee, which she places on the stool below the sofa.*)

JAMES. You'll have some coffee, won't you?

PRESTON. Thank you.

(ALICE *lights the lamp under the coffee.* JAMES *moves to the table Up Left and picks up the box of cigars.*)

JANET. There's a telephone message just come through from the Vicarage, madam. The Vicar wants to know if he can come and see Mr. Winter for a few minutes.

ALICE. Oh dear! What shall I say, James?

JAMES. (*Moving Down Left Center.*) My dear, it doesn't make very much difference what you say. If the Vicar has made up his mind to come—he'll come, unless he forgets on the way. Did he say what he wanted, Janet?

JANET. He said he'd forgotten for the moment, sir, but he'd remember by the time he got here.

JAMES. I very much doubt it. However, send him along.

JANET. Thank you, sir.

(JANET *exits Up Center.*)

JAMES. (*Offering the cigar box to* PRESTON.) A cigar?

PRESTON. A cigarette, I think, if you don't mind.

JAMES. Pat. (*He replaces the cigar box on the table Up Left.*)

(PAT *crosses to the table Center, picks up the box of cigarettes and moves to Left of* PRESTON.)

ACT I WHITE SHEEP OF THE FAMILY

ALICE. You know our Vicar, Commissioner?

PRESTON. Indeed I do.

ALICE. I'm afraid he is getting a little past it.

PAT. Does that matter in the Church? (*She offers* PRESTON *a cigarette.*) I thought it was like the House of Lords.

PRESTON. (*To* PAT; *taking a cigarette.*) Thank you. (*To* ALICE.) Perhaps I ought to tell you what I've come for. Actually, the Vicar's mixed up in it. (*To* JAMES.) Has he mentioned it to you?

(PAT *replaces the cigarette box on the table Center, then sits in the armchair Right Center.* PRESTON *lights his cigarette.*)

JAMES. (*Sitting in the armchair Left Center.*) The Vicar has mentioned a great many things to me—none of them relevant—few of them even coherent.

PRESTON. No—quite. I expected it slipped his memory. So I thought I'd better see you, as one of his churchwardens. The Vicar has kindly agreed to devote the proceeds of a special collection to the Discharged Prisoners Aid Society. You've heard of it, of course?

JAMES. Oh, yes.

PRESTON. A very deserving cause. We like to do what we can—the Police, I mean.

JAMES. Only reasonable. If you put a man away, it's only fair to help him to get back.

PRESTON. Quite. Besides, it may save us the trouble of having to put him away again. We don't particularly enjoy it.

JAMES. Neither does he, I imagine.

PRESTON. You'd be surprised. Some of the old lags are never happy out of prison. However, we are very grateful to the Vicar—and to you, Mr. Winter.

JAMES. I'm grateful to you, for telling me. I should never have heard about it from the Vicar.

ALICE. (*Pouring coffee.*) Sugar, Commissioner?

PRESTON. No sugar, thank you.

JAMES. (*Rising.*) Now that you have told me, I'll see the Vicar doesn't send the collection to the Home for Lost Dogs. (*He crosses to* ALICE *and takes a cup of coffee from her.*) Thank you, my dear. And if there's anything else I can do, I'll do it with pleasure. (*He resumes his seat in the armchair Left Center.*)

PRESTON. Thank you.

PAT. Now tell me all the latest news about crime.

PRESTON. (*Amused.*) What sort of crime?

PAT. Oh, the things one dials nine-nine-nine for, and all that.

PRESTON. You'd be disappointed, I'm afraid. Crime's a dull business, really. Not all that it's cracked up to be, so to speak. Criminals are stupid people, as a rule. They go round and round in the same old groove.

PAT. You may not know it, but you're wrecking all my girlish dreams.

JAMES. Are all criminals so stupid?

PRESTON. Oh no. Occasionally we have to deal with quite an original character. Did you read in the paper about the Duke of Troon's house being burgled last week? Some valuable family heirlooms were stolen.

JAMES. But that's a fairly normal thing to happen these days.

PRESTON. Yes. But now comes the abnormal. The jewels were returned, two days later, by post.

PAT. Why?

PRESTON. That's what I should like to know.

JAMES. Perhaps the burglar discovered they were fakes.

PRESTON. They weren't. But that's not all. Exactly the same thing happened two days later, at a flat in Park Lane. This time the jewels were returned by hand.

JAMES. By hand?

PAT. Don't say the burglar rang the bell and handed them in.

PRESTON. All we know is that the hall-porter found them lying on his desk, in a neat parcel, two days later.

PAT. You think it was the same burglar each time?

PRESTON. Almost certainly.

ACT I WHITE SHEEP OF THE FAMILY 13

PAT. He must be potty!

ALICE. But supposing you did catch him, can you do anything to him? After all, he did return the jewels. I think it was rather nice of him.

PRESTON. The actual stealing doesn't matter. We could always get him for breaking and entering. What I want to ask him is why he returned the stuff.

JAMES. Perhaps he was working to rule.

PRESTON. Who knows! Well, I've talked shop long enough. I'm sorry. (*He rises.*) I must be going back to the Yard.

(ALICE, PAT *and* JAMES *rise.*)

JAMES. The police never sleep, eh?

PRESTON. They're often caught napping. Good-bye, Mrs. Winter.

ALICE. Good-bye, Commissioner.

PRESTON. Thank you for the coffee. Good-bye, Miss Winter. You look as though you're going out.

PAT. Yes, the Opera.

PRESTON. I hope you enjoy it. My daughter's at *Covent Garden* tonight, I believe. (*To* JAMES.) Good night, sir. And many thanks.

JAMES. You won't stay and have a word with the Vicar? He'll be here any minute.

PRESTON. No, I don't think so, thanks.

(*They all laugh.*)

PAT. (*Moving to the door Up Center.*) I'll see you out.

PRESTON. (*Moving to the door Up Center.*) Thank you. Good night.

JAMES. Good night.

ALICE. Good night. (PAT *and* PRESTON *exit Up Center.* JAMES *picks up the "Evening Standard," sits in the armchair Left Center and opens the paper. She sits on the sofa.*) What a nice man. Funny about all those jewels being returned.

JAMES. Why funny?

ALICE. Well, it seems so silly to take all that trouble for nothing. You might just as well stay at home and look at television.

JAMES. Quite so. (PAT *enters Up Center. To* PAT.) Isn't it about time you started for *Covent Garden,* my dear?

PAT. (*Moving to Right of the sofa.*) No hurry. (*She helps herself to a cup of coffee.*) There's no point in getting there before the second interval.

JAMES. Oh no, of course not.

ALICE. Are you going on anywhere afterwards, darling?

PAT. (*Crossing to the fireplace.*) To supper, and a little dancing.

ALICE. Who with?

PAT. Ronnie.

JAMES. Young Ronnie Devenish? A nice lad. Let me see—his father should be coming out any time now.

ALICE. (*Reprovingly.*) James!

JAMES. Why not? He got ten years in nineteen forty-four. I've no doubt his conduct has been exemplary. So he should be out any day.

ALICE. I don't think it's a thing you should talk about.

JAMES. It's a thing that might happen to any of us.

ALICE. Now, James, that's not at all a nice thing to say.

JAMES. It's not at all a nice thing to contemplate.

PAT. What was he like?

JAMES. Who?

PAT. Ronnie's father.

JAMES. Oh, charming. Absolutely charming. But he would not listen to reason. I warned him. It was over some new kind of confidence trick. Not a very good one, apparently.

PAT. You mean he asked for it?

JAMES. He practically went down on his knees and prayed for it. And his prayer was answered.

ALICE. Really, James. If you can't talk about something more cheerful, read your paper. Surely we've had enough crime for one evening.

PAT. (*Crossing to Left of the sofa; rather diffidently.*) I say, Father—talking of Ronnie—I saw Peter yesterday.

JAMES. Oh.

ALICE. You never told me. How was he looking?

PAT. All right.

ALICE. I do hope he's getting enough to eat.

JAMES. My dear, just because your son chooses to leave home and lead his own life, it doesn't mean he's forgotten how to order a meal. (*To* PAT.) Was he alone?

PAT. He had a girl with him.

ALICE. Oh dear!

JAMES. Not a very unusual thing to happen to a young man.

ALICE. What sort of girl?

PAT. She looked right enough. Pretty, too.

JAMES. Did you speak to him?

PAT. No. I was busy.

JAMES. (*Understandingly.*) Oh yes, of course.

PAT. He didn't see me.

ALICE. All the same, dear, I do think you might have asked him where he was living.

JAMES. (*Kindly.*) If Peter wants us to know where he's living, he'll tell us. In the meantime, he's perfectly capable of looking after himself.

PAT. Father, why did Peter walk out on us?

JAMES. Ask your mother, my dear. He didn't confide in me.

ALICE. He didn't tell me a thing. Just went.

PAT. He's been a bit peculiar for some time.

ALICE. (*Anxiously.*) How do you mean, dear—peculiar?

JAMES. Geniuses often appear eccentric to normal folk. And Peter is a genius, in his own line.

PAT. When did he last do a job?

JAMES. Several months ago. But that's nothing to go by. Peter doesn't believe in flooding the market. I think he's quite right.

PAT. You don't think he's weakening, do you?

JAMES. Weakening?

PAT. Letting the firm down.

JAMES. Good heavens, no!

ALICE. (*Shocked.*) Peter would never do a thing like that, dear.

PAT. (*Moving above the table Center.*) I wonder.

JAMES. No. Family tradition means just as much to Peter as it does to me—or any of us. He'd never let us down.

PAT. I wouldn't put it past him, all the same. He's been gone six weeks, and not a word. He might have been in prison for all we know.

ALICE. Oh no, dear—not Peter.

PAT. I know it's not likely, but . . .

JAMES. (*Looking up from his paper.*) Nobody's been in prison in our family for three generations.

PAT. What about Uncle Clarence?

JAMES. Your Uncle Clarence was on your mother's side.

ALICE. Now, James, you can't blame me for that.

JAMES. I don't blame you, my dear. Your brother was unfortunate, that's all. Still, it isn't a nice thing to happen in a family like ours. It destroys confidence. Peter knows that as well as I do.

PAT. Yes, but what's he doing? And whatever it is, why couldn't he do it here?

JAMES. Possibly the young lady might be able to inform you.

PAT. He's got snatched up, that's what it is. It's all right, Mother—I know what girls are.

ALICE. But Peter has never been interested in girls, dear.

PAT. It's funny how all mothers think that. (*The front doorbell rings. She moves to the door Up Center.*) That'll be the Vicar. I'll go. (*PAT exits.*)

ALICE. What an hour to call!

JAMES. Time means nothing to our dear Vicar—and less with each succeeding year. I wonder what he wants this time.

ACT I WHITE SHEEP OF THE FAMILY

ALICE. I wonder if he knows himself.
JAMES. I shouldn't think so.
ALICE. Well, you are his churchwarden. I expect he wants to ask your advice about something.
JAMES. Vicars don't come to churchwardens for advice, dear. Merely for confirmation of what they've already decided upon.

(PAT *and the* VICAR *enter Up Center. The* VICAR *is very old and absent-minded, but guileless and quite charming.* ALICE *rises.* JAMES *rises and stands with his back to the fire.*)

PAT. Here's the Vicar to see us, Mother.
VICAR. (*Crossing to Left Center.*) Ah, how do you do, Mrs. Winter? How do you do?
ALICE. How do you do, Vicar?

(PAT *moves below the table Right Center.*)

VICAR. I'm very well, I think. Yes—I think so. If I weren't I should know about it, shouldn't I?

(ALICE *sits on the sofa at the Right end.*)

JAMES. Anyhow, we're delighted to see you, Vicar.
VICAR. That's very kind of you. Let me see—you telephoned me about—er—what was it?
JAMES. No, it was you who telephoned me.
VICAR. Was it? Probably it was. (*He crosses to Left of* PAT.) How do you do, my dear?
PAT. We met outside, do you remember?
VICAR. To be sure. Forgive me. I must have mistaken you for your sister.
PAT. I haven't got a sister, Vicar.
VICAR. (*Concerned.*) Haven't you? Oh dear—how sad. I hadn't heard.
PAT. (*Smiling.*) Let me take your hat.

VICAR. (*Looking with surprise at his hat.*) Oh. Oh, thank you. (*He hands the hat to* PAT.)

(PAT *puts the hat on the table Right Center.*)

JAMES. I'm sorry you didn't look in sooner, Vicar. You have just missed a friend of yours, John Preston.

VICAR. (*Turning and moving below the sofa.*) Preston? Let me think.

PAT. From Scotland Yard.

VICAR. I should have liked to meet him. My poor dear wife had quite a number of relatives from there. A beautiful country. The land of mountain and flood, Sir Walter Scott . . .

JAMES. Not Scotland, Vicar. Scotland Yard. Our visitor was a policeman.

VICAR. A policeman?

PAT. A copper.

VICAR. Oh—a policeman. A splendid force! Was it Mr. Jobson, by any chance?

JAMES. Jobson?

VICAR. It may be Dobson, or even Hobson. He patrols our square at night. My cook thinks very highly of him.

JAMES. (*Patiently.*) I was referring to our mutual friend, Assistant Commissioner John Preston.

VICAR. Ah, to be sure.

ALICE. Sit down and have a cup of coffee, Vicar.

VICAR. Oh, thank you. (*He crosses to* JAMES.) I can't tell you how glad I am that—er . . .

(JAMES *moves to the table Up Left and picks up the box of cigars.*)

ALICE. Black or white, Vicar?

VICAR. Yes, please. Er—what was I saying?

JAMES. (*Moving to Left of the armchair Left Center.*) Sit down, Vicar. (*He indicates the armchair.*)

VICAR. Oh, thank you. (*He sits hurriedly.*) But this is your chair, is it not?

ACT I WHITE SHEEP OF THE FAMILY 19

JAMES. No, no. Very happy to see you in it.
VICAR. Oh, thank you.
JAMES. Have a cigar.

(PAT *picks up the cup of coffee for the* VICAR *and crosses to Right of him.*)

VICAR. (*Taking a cigar.*) Ah! An unaccustomed luxury.
PAT. (*Putting the cup on the table Right of the armchair.*) Your coffee, Vicar.
VICAR. Thank you, my dear.
PAT. (*Indicating the cigar.*) Let me pierce it for you.
VICAR. That's very kind of you.
JAMES. Be careful. Don't crack it.
PAT. As if I would!
VICAR. You talk as if it were a crib.
PAT. A what?
VICAR. A crib. To crack a crib is a technical term employed by the criminal classes to denote burglary. At least, so I am told.

(PAT *gets the matches from the table Center.*)

JAMES. (*Replacing the cigars on the table Up Left.*) Who told you that?
VICAR. The Archdeacon. (PAT *strikes a match and holds it while the* VICAR *puffs at his cigar.*) Thank you, my dear. Now how did we come to be talking about burglars? Really, this is an extremely pleasant cigar.

(PAT *sits on the sofa at Left end.*)

JAMES. (*Moving to the armchair Down Left and sitting.*) Very unusual in these days of austerity.
VICAR. Where do you get them, if I may ask?
JAMES. Those? Oh, I stole them.
VICAR. (*Laughing.*) Very good. What a pity you can't steal some for me.
JAMES. I will with pleasure. Any particular brand?

VICAR. (*Suddenly.*) Ah, now I know why I mentioned burglars. I can't tell you how glad I am that Janet is with a family such as this. Here she is safe—secure—free from all undesirable influences. (*He absently picks up his cup of coffee.*)

ALICE. We're very glad to have her.

VICAR. Her parents. Not very . . . (*He shakes his head.*) The father's in Dartmouth, you know.

JAMES. I expect you mean Dartmoor.

VICAR. Oh, do I? Probably. I've never been there myself.

ALICE. It's all very sad. Don't forget your coffee, Vicar.

VICAR. Coffee? No thank you—no coffee.

PAT. Don't let it get cold.

VICAR. (*Looking with surprise at the cup in his hand.*) Oh! No, of course not. (*He drinks.*)

(PAT *rises.*)

JAMES. (*Rising.*) I'm sorry we can't offer you a rubber tonight, Vicar. Pat's going to the Opera.

VICAR. Oh, I couldn't stay—really. (*He puts down his coffee-cup and leans back in his chair.*) I only dropped in to—er . . . (*He pauses and thinks.*) I must have come for something.

JAMES. Some parish matter? The Choir Picnic?

ALICE. The Dorcas Society?

PAT. The Young Women's Guild?

VICAR. No, I don't think so.

ALICE. (*Rising.*) I know—it's a subscription for something.

VICAR. Oh, is it? For what?

ALICE. You'll remember presently.

VICAR. You know, sometimes I think my memory's not what it was.

JAMES. I haven't noticed any difference whatever, Vicar.

VICAR. Oh, thank you. Yes, that's what the girl needed.

ACT I　WHITE SHEEP OF THE FAMILY　21

A place with a thoroughly respectable family. I can't tell you how glad I am.

ALICE. (*Gently.*) You have told us, Vicar.

VICAR. Oh, have I? I mustn't start repeating myself. That's a sign of old age, you know.

ALICE. Not at all. You merely came to ask how Janet was getting on.

VICAR. Did I? I don't think so. There was something else. I shall recollect presently. (JAMES *and* PAT *resume their seats.*) But I won't stop. (*He rises.* JAMES *and* PAT *rise.*) It must be getting late. (*He feels in his pocket.*) Oh dear, I've left my watch at home. (*He pauses.*) In any case, I only meant to look in for a moment—just to tell you—er—(PAT *crosses and stands above the table Right Center.*)—whatever it was. I have to call on Mrs. —er—dear, dear, I know her name perfectly well. (*He crosses to* ALICE.) She's had the same pew for thirty years. Something like Prendergast.

ALICE. Mrs. Wedderburn?

VICAR. That's it. Mrs. Wedderburn! Of course. Poor woman, her husband's been very ill, you know.

JAMES. He died just a year ago, Vicar.

VICAR. Did he? Oh yes, of course he did. I'm very glad you mentioned it. Poor lady. I must go and speak a few words of comfort to her.

PAT. But it was last year, Vicar.

VICAR. Last year. (*He nods.*) I remember it all now. Influenza, wasn't it?

ALICE. A railway accident.

VICAR. A railway accident, of course. Well, good night, Mrs. Wedderburn, good night. (*He shakes hands with* ALICE. ALICE *resumes her seat on the sofa. He crosses above the sofa to* PAT.) Good night, Miss—er . . . Oh, have you been to a party? I hope you enjoyed it.

PAT. No, I'm going to the Opera.

VICAR. Oh, very nice. (*He moves to the door Up Center.*) I can let myself out.

JAMES. (*Crossing to the* VICAR.) I'll come with you.

VICAR. You are too kind. Good night. Good night. (*He turns to the door.*)

PAT. (*Picking up the* VICAR'S *hat and moving quickly to him.*) Oh, Vicar, your hat. (*As she picks up the hat from the table Right Center she also picks up the watch previously concealed on the table.*)

VICAR. (*Taking his hat.*) Oh, thank you. Good night again. Good night.

(*The* VICAR *and* JAMES *exit Up Center.* PAT *looks at the watch and giggles.*)

ALICE. What's that you've got?

PAT. (*Moving Down Right.*) I'm afraid it's the Vicar's watch.

ALICE. Pat! That's very naughty of you. After all, the Vicar's a *friend*.

PAT. I know. I wasn't thinking what I was doing.

ALICE. No, really, darling.

PAT. Stupid of me. I sometimes do it without thinking—especially when it's so easy. (*She laughs.*) If everybody was like the Vicar, what a world.

(JAMES *enters Up Center and moves to Right of the sofa.*)

ALICE. Look what Pat's got.

PAT. I'm sorry, Father. It was just sheer absentmindedness.

JAMES. Oh dear. No—you shouldn't have done that, Pat.

PAT. I know. I wasn't thinking.

JAMES. Strangers are one thing—that's just business. But not friends of the family.

ALICE. Especially the clergy, dear.

PAT. It was—I don't know—it was just instinct.

JAMES. Pat. There's no-one in London has quicker fingers than you have, and I'm proud of you, darling. But in a profession like ours—particularly in a profession like ours—one must have standards. The general public is the general public, and must look after itself. Friends are friends. Besides, it isn't a very good one. (*He crosses to the armchair Left Center, sits and picks up his newspaper.*)

PAT. Fancy him talking about cracking cribs. (*She laughs.*) Did you really get those cigars from a job?

JAMES. All the shops were shut. What else could I do?

ALICE. All the same, James, I don't think you should have told him that you stole them.

JAMES. Why not? It's perfectly true.

(PAT *crosses to the desk, quietly hides the watch in the desk drawer, then picks up a magazine.*)

ALICE. It isn't a word I like to hear you use. My grandfather was a man very highly respected in his profession—and he would never have dreamed of regarding anything as stolen.

JAMES. He was in a different line of business altogether; he was a forger.

ALICE. (*Correcting him gently.*) An engraver, dear.

JAMES. I beg your pardon. (*He commences to read his paper.*)

ALICE. Though of course, as he pointed out, he never took money from anyone. He simply helped people by putting more of it into circulation.

PAT. Nobody could object to that.

ALICE. Nobody did, dear, until they found him out. Then of course, they didn't even try to understand.

PAT. (*Moving Down Right Center.*) He went inside, didn't he?

ALICE. Yes, dear. I wish you could have known him. He was a charming man—and his work was really beautiful.

PAT. Peter's work's pretty good.

ALICE. Peter's got some of his great-grandfather's talent, I grant you. But when Jim the Penman—that's what they called him—when Jim the Penman was forging a note, it might have been an R.A. painting an Academy picture. He put his whole soul into it.

JAMES. Pat. Pass me the scissors, will you, please.

(PAT *moves to the table Center, takes the scissors from the work-basket, crosses to* JAMES *and stands Right of him.*)

PAT. Found something?

JAMES. Yes. Rather a good account of last night's work. The usual journalistic inaccuracies, of course. (*He reads.*) "It is thought that this audacious robbery must have been effected by the employment of an accomplice within the house itself." (*He takes the scissors from* PAT *and cuts out the report.*)

ALICE. Why should they think it was an inside job?

PAT. Was it an inside job, Father?

JAMES. Certainly not. I like "audacious" much better than "daring" or "impudent." The English of our popular press is improving. So is the intelligence of the police. (*He puts the scissors on the table Right of his chair.*) Listen to this. (*He reads.*) "The police are of the opinion that this audacious—" audacious again, you see—"this audacious burglary is the work of the same gang which only last week got away with twenty thousand pounds' worth of jewellery from the town house of the Dowager Lady Lulworth."

PAT. You'll have to change your methods.

JAMES. Why should I? Technique is style. The distinctive artist can always be recognized by it. But they grossly over-estimate the value of Lady Lulworth's rather second-rate diamonds. (*He rises and moves above the sofa to the table Center.*) Still, on the whole it's a complimentary notice. I think we'll put it in the book.

ALICE. You're a vain old man, James.

(PAT *folds the remains of the newspaper, puts it on the table Center, then moves to the bookshelves Up Left Center, swings open a section of it, takes a news-*

ACT I WHITE SHEEP OF THE FAMILY 25

cutting book and a small pot of paste out of the cupboard behind the bookshelves, and places them on the table Center.)

JAMES. Vain, possibly. But I object strongly to "old." Listen to this. (*He reads.*) "The burglar or burglars effected an entrance—" isn't it extraordinary how a burglar never merely gets in anywhere? I suppose one of these days I shall "effect an entrance" into heaven—"effected an entrance in a way which indicated careful preparation and considerable physical activity."

PAT. (*Standing Left of* JAMES *at the table Center.*) What did you do really?

JAMES. Went in through the back door. But before leaving I took the precaution of forcing a second-floor window and breaking a few strands of ivy outside it. It's only fair to give the police something to stimulate their imagination.

(*While* JAMES *helps,* PAT *pastes the cutting into the book.*)

PAT. And then?

JAMES. Then I came out through the front door—or should I say effected an exit—and locked it after me. (*The front doorbell rings long and loudly.*) All very quiet and respectable. Was that a ring at the bell?

PAT. Yes. It sounds like your friend Sam Jackson. I'd know his signature tune anywhere.

JAMES. I was expecting him. In fact, I asked him to call. (PAT *exits Up Center.* ALICE *grimaces.*) Now, my dear, why that wry face?

ALICE. Your friend Mr. Jackson. Must we have him here?

JAMES. He's indispensable. That's the sole reason why I employ him.

ALICE. But he's so vulgar and so conceited. Do you know, he thinks he's cleverer than you are?

JAMES. And isn't he?

ALICE. Oh, darling! You're the cleverest of them all.

JAMES. (*Sitting on the sofa Right of* ALICE; *smiling.*) You're not without a pretty gift yourself.

ALICE. That's nothing.

JAMES. Isn't it? Who was it slipped into a thousand-guinea mink coat in that fur shop in Knightsbridge, and then calmly walked out in it?

ALICE. The only anxious moment was standing outside, waiting for a taxi.

JAMES. (*Putting his arm around her.*) I should have run like a rabbit.

ALICE. Of course, dear, you might have looked a little conspicuous in mink.

(*They both laugh happily.* PAT *enters Up Center.*)

PAT. Walk right in, Sam. The gang's all here.

(SAM JACKSON *enters Up Center. He is middle-aged and well-dressed, and looks rather like a prosperous stockbroker. He cultivates a certain refinement of manner, but whenever he gets excited, which he frequently does, he relapses into an ordinary, second-rate crook.* JAMES *rises, crosses and stands with his back to the fireplace.* PAT *stands above the table Center.*)

SAM. (*Moving Down Left Center.*) Good evening, everybody. How well you're looking, Mrs. Winter. And how is my old friend James? (*He shakes hands with* ALICE *and* JAMES.)

ALICE. We haven't seen you lately, Mr. Jackson.

SAM. No. (*Rather grandly.*) I had to slip over in the Continong, to have a look at our Paris and Amsterdam branches. Paris—(*He gives the thumbs down gesture.*) not what it was. Or else it's me. Getting older, perhaps.

JAMES. What about Amsterdam?

SAM. You can have Amsterdam on a plate as far as I'm concerned. A dead-and-alive hole if ever there was

ACT I WHITE SHEEP OF THE FAMILY 27

one. (*He resumes his refined manner.*) Still, when all's said and done, Amsterdam is the headquarters of the diamond-cutting-and-setting business, so to Amsterdam one has to go every now and again. A bore, but there it is, old boy.

JAMES. Never mind Amsterdam. What we want is news from nearer home. Pat, give Sam a drink. (PAT *crosses to the cabinet Down Right and pours a drink for* SAM. SAM *crosses and sits in the armchair Right Center.*) How is business in Hatton Garden? That's what really interests us.

SAM. Are you referring to business in the front office or the little back room?

JAMES. (*Crossing to Left of Sam; smiling.*) You can have your front office on a nice silver salver, hall marked.

SAM. (*Smiling.*) Yes, I get you! You want to hear all about my junior colleagues.

PAT. The wide boys. (*She pours a drink for* JAMES.)

JAMES. I hope they've been behaving with discretion—keeping on the right side of the fence, so to speak. (PAT *laughs.*)

SAM. (*Annoyed.*) Now really, James, I can enjoy a joke with the next man, but I do not like being called a fence. It's not true and it's not etiquette. (*He pronounces the word as spelt.*) I've spoken to you about it before. There are no fences in Hatton Garden.

PAT. Oh? What do they call themselves? Unofficial Receivers?

SAM. International Brokers. Don't we all have to live up to our surroundings in this world?

JAMES. You certainly do—my goodness, yes. (*He looks* SAM *up and down.*) Not a hair out of place, and a carnation in your buttonhole.

SAM. (*Flattered.*) And rightly.

(PAT *picks up the two drinks, moves below the table Right Center, hands one drink to* SAM *and the other to* JAMES, *then returns to the cabinet and pours a drink for herself.*)

PAT. Here you are, Sam. I'm sorry we have no champagne on tap this evening.

SAM. That's right, my angel. This'll do for yours truly. (*He raises his glass.*) Well, the old toast—"Ourselves." And a good run for our money.

JAMES. And may we never have to run too fast. (PAT, SAM *and* JAMES *drink. He crosses to the desk and puts his drink on it.*) Now, shall we talk business? (*He opens the panel below the window and reveals the safe behind it.*)

SAM. That's what I'm here for. Have you by any chance got a little present for me from the Dowager Marchioness of Lulworth?

JAMES. (*Working on the combination lock of the safe.*) How did you guess that was me?

SAM. (*Rising and moving above the table Right Center.*) How do I know it's a duck, when it quacks—as it were.

(JAMES *takes an old cigar box from the safe, puts the box on the table Right Center, opens it and takes out a smaller box which he retains.*)

JAMES. Well, there's the stuff—and more. I've been very busy the last week or two. What do you think of it?

(SAM *takes a jeweller's glass from his pocket, picks up some of the jewellery from the box and examines it.*)

SAM. (*Presently.*) Oh, dear, dear, dear! I did think her ladyship would have something better than this.

(PAT *sits on the stool at the desk and looks into her bag.*)

JAMES. And she had the effrontery to tell the police it was worth twenty thousand pounds. I shall never believe a member of the aristocracy again.

SAM. Crooks, all of them.

JAMES. (*Taking a diamond necklace from the small*

box.) What about these little fellows? (*He hands the necklace to* SAM.)

SAM. (*Excitedly.*) Blimey! Where did you get these? (*He puts the jeweller's glass in his eye and looks at the necklace.*)

JAMES. Do you know them?

SAM. Know them! So 'elp me bob! (*He pulls himself up.*) I assure you, everybody knows them. I thought they were in New York.

JAMES. They arrived in London last week.

SAM. Who put you wise?

JAMES. A friend of mine in the *Queen Mary*.

SAM. I wish I had your contacts. And you got in on the ground floor, eh?

JAMES. That's exactly what I did.

SAM. I'll take these with me and see what I can afford to pay you for them.

JAMES. Afford?

SAM. They're pretty well known. They may have to go abroad. Very difficult to place here.

JAMES. Oh, I think you'll manage it all right. It'd be an awful shame if I had to change my international broker. (*He moves and stands above the sofa.*)

SAM. Yeees. (*He puts the jewels in his pocket.*)

(PAT *takes a bracelet from her handbag, rises and hands the bracelet to* SAM.)

PAT. How do you like this?

SAM. (*Enthusiastically.*) Well! (*He corrects himself.*) H'm—fairly good. Who was wearing it?

(ALICE *rises, moves to the armchair Left Center, picks up the cushion from it and commences to put on the new cover.*)

PAT. A fat woman at the Mansion House two nights ago. A duchess probably—with a tiara.

SAM. Pity.

PAT. What do you mean—a pity?

SAM. Pity you didn't bring the tiara as well.

PAT. I should have brought her wig with it, if I had, and she might have noticed. What's it worth?

SAM. Oh, I dunno. About five hundred.

PAT. And you'll give me fifty for it, I suppose.

SAM. No. Because I'm a friend of the family, and you're a special pet of mine, I'll give you (*He catches* JAMES's *eye.*) a hundred.

PAT. Done! (*She holds out her hand.*)

(JAMES *crosses to* ALICE *and assists her with the cushion cover.*)

SAM. (*Taking a packet of notes from his pocket.*) Right. Here you are. (*He hands the notes to* PAT.) Count them.

PAT. I wouldn't be so insulting. But I'm not going to have that one. (*She removes one note from the packet.*)

SAM. Why not?

PAT. Really, Sam, I'm surprised at you. That's one of Peter's. (*She crosses to* JAMES.) Isn't it, Father? (*She hands the note to* JAMES.)

JAMES. (*Holding the note up to the light.*) Yes, that's Peter's, all right. Good, isn't it?

SAM. (*Crossing to* JAMES *and taking the note from him.*) And I never spotted it. I must be getting wall-eyed. I apologize. But if you will have a brother as clever as Peter, what do you expect? You must be pretty proud of him.

JAMES. Yes. Ever since he was a boy, I knew Peter would make money.

ALICE. (*Calmly.*) Of course he gets it from my side of the family. (*She resumes work on the cushion cover.*)

SAM. (*Taking another note from his pocket and giving it to* PAT.) There you are, love. That one is all right, I think.

PAT. (*Examining the note.*) It'll do.

SAM. If you find any more of Peter's in that lot, I'll change them for you.

PAT. I'll take care of that, my dear. (*She crosses to the desk and during the following speeches, carefully examines the notes.*)

SAM. (*Crossing to the cabinet Right.*) James, there's another small matter I've got to discuss with you. (*He helps himself to a drink.*) It's been rather on my mind.

ALICE. Would you like me to take my work into another room?

SAM. (*Crossing to the fireplace.*) No; I think you ought to be in on this, too. It concerns the credit of the whole profession, in a manner of speaking.

ALICE. (*Sitting on the sofa at the right end; amiably.*) Very well.

JAMES. (*Sitting on the sofa at the left end.*) What is on your mind, Sam?

SAM. A mystery. It's been downright worrying me. Last Monday night the Duke of Troon's house in Portman Square was broken into, and a lot of valuable family heirlooms got pinched.

JAMES. (*Loudly.*) Not guilty, my lord.

SAM. You don't have to reassure me on that point, my boy.

JAMES. Thank you. Why not?

SAM. Well, if you'd been the one that did the job you'd have brought the proceeds straight to me, as usual. But you didn't. That means that somebody else has got the stuff. But who? I've enquired amongst most of my—er—colleagues . . .

JAMES. The back-room boys?

SAM. That's right; and no-one has been approached. I've talked to Paris and Amsterdam too, and nothing's arrived there. What's become of the stuff?

JAMES. Oddly enough, I can answer that question. The jewellery was returned to the Duke of Troon by registered post.

SAM. Who told you that?

JAMES. A friend of mine at Scotland Yard.

(ALICE *rises, crosses to the armchair down Left and fits the cover on to the cushion.*)

SAM. Come orf it! What I mean to say is—let's be serious, old man.

JAMES. An Assistant Commissioner, if you must know.

(ALICE *sits in the armchair Down Left.*)

SAM. An Assistant Commissioner? (*He crosses to left of* JAMES.) Scotland Yard!

JAMES. We're both on the council of the Church Lads' Brigade.

SAM. Oh! Well, that's different. Of course, it might be just a case of cold feet. (*He crosses to the fireplace.*) Well-known family heirlooms: too hot to handle. I could have handled them for him, if he'd given me the chance. But what does he go and do? Sends them back—by post—and then wastes good money registering them.

ALICE. I think it was rather nice of him. After all, if he didn't want them himself, the owner had next claim, didn't he?

SAM. If you ask me, there are too many amateurs nowadays trying to muscle in on our racket.

JAMES. I agree, but that's not the end of the mystery. Two nights later a very rich woman, Mrs. Brainton West—she lives in one of those luxury flats in Park Lane—was robbed of ten thousand pounds' worth of diamonds.

SAM. So I heard.

JAMES. How?

SAM. Through the usual channels. Ah, but diamonds—they're easy to get rid of. They'll be on the market soon enough.

JAMES. They won't, you know.

SAM. Why not?

JAMES. They were returned too.

SAM. (*Crossing to* JAMES.) Is this guy going to make a habit of this?

ACT I WHITE SHEEP OF THE FAMILY 33

JAMES. Time will show.

SAM. (*Excitedly.*) But blimey O'Reilly, what's going to become of *us!* It's taking the bread out of our mouths. And what good does it do him, anyway? It just doesn't make sense.

JAMES. I couldn't agree more.

SAM. (*Struck by a sudden thought.*) Mr. Winter, you seem to be very well informed, so to speak, about this new racket. Now—I know you enjoy a little joke every now and again; it's only natural, with your sense of humour. But are you quite sure you haven't been having a bit of fun at our expense? Because, if so—well . . .

JAMES. (*Rising; with dignity.*) Jackson. My family has been in this profession—father and son—for four generations. I am not an amateur. I do not mix business with fun.

SAM. (*Abjectly.*) Sorry, Governor! I shouldn't have suggested it. I take it all back. No hard feelings, eh?

JAMES. (*Moving Up Center.*) No hard feelings at all. (*He replaces the book of cuttings in the cupboard behind the bookshelves.*)

PAT. (*Crossing to* SAM.) Really, Sam! This is very careless of you. I've found five more of these notes— three of them Peter's. The other two look like Inky Joe's.

(ALICE *rises.* JAMES *moves Down Left of* SAM.)

SAM. (*Taking the notes from* PAT.) Dear, dear, dear! Fancy me being as careless as that.

PAT. You owe me five pounds.

SAM. (*Glancing at* JAMES.) Of course, I was forgetting.

PAT. Oh no, you weren't. Come on.

SAM. (*Taking a note from his pocket and handing it to* PAT.) There you are, love. There's a fiver for you. (*He places the five one-pound notes on the coffee tray.*)

PAT. Thank you.

(JAMES *sits in the armchair Left Center.*)

SAM. It's a pleasure. (*The front doorbell rings.* PAT *crosses to the door Up Center and exits. He crosses and stands with his back to the fire.*) You know—I've been thinking, and I see trouble coming in more ways than one over this business. This by-return-of-post business. What are the rank-and-file going to say about it? The small timers. They take a pride in their work. (ALICE *crosses and sits on the sofa.*) If this sort of thing goes on, and the news gets about, why, the whole profession's going to become a laughing-stock. And they won't like that, you know; they're artists. They're sensitive. Blimey, it's enough to make some of 'em go straight.

(*Voices are heard off.*)

ALICE. Oh dear—it's the Vicar again.
SAM. (*Alarmed.*) The Vicar—what—a dodger? That's nearly as bad as a cop.

(PAT *and the* VICAR *enter Up Center.* PAT *moves Down Right Center. The* VICAR *moves Left of the sofa.* JAMES *rises.* SAM *moves Down Left.*)

PAT. The Vicar, Mother.
VICAR. (*Shaking hands with* ALICE.) Ah, good evening. How fortunate I am to find you at home. (*He turns and moves quickly to* SAM.) And you, Mr. Winter. (*He suddenly realizes his mistake.*) Oh, I beg your pardon—I am intruding.
JAMES. No, no, no. Come in. This is Mr. Sam Jackson.
VICAR. (*Shaking hands with* SAM.) Oh, how do you do, Mr. Samson?
SAM. Jackson. (*In his most refined voice.*) I'm sure I'm very pleased to meet you.
VICAR. (*Peering at* SAM.) Your face is vaguely familiar. Let me think. You are not one of my parishioners.
SAM. (*Elegantly.*) No. I reside in another district, I fear.

VICAR. But I feel sure I've met you—perhaps in one of your business capacities.

SAM. (*With a quick look at* JAMES; *startled.*) Which of them?

(PAT *sits in the armchair Right Center.*)

VICAR. Which of them? All business is a mystery to me. (*He moves thoughtfully to Left of the coffee stool.*) Business—big business. How fascinating it all sounds. Yet after all, what is money? (*He picks up the notes from the coffee tray.*) These notes, for example—these insignificant scraps of paper. Have they any real value?

SAM. None whatever.

VICAR. And yet, worthless though they appear, they might be of real use in the missionary field. Whenever I see money lying about, I always say to the owner, "If you have so little use for your shillings and pence, I can use them." Why, I believe you left these here on purpose.

JAMES. My dear Vicar, if they were mine you could have them with pleasure. They belong to Mr. Jackson.

VICAR. Only worthless pieces of paper, you know, Mr. Jackson.

SAM. You said it! (*Hastily.*) I mean, I agree, in principle.

VICAR. And yet, in a sense, I have no doubt they represent a lot of hard labour.

SAM. (*With a look at* JAMES.) They might, they might.

VICAR. But what could not be done with them if properly used.

SAM. (*Politely.*) If you so desire it, they are yours.

VICAR. That is very generous of you, my dear sir. Yes, very generous. You will not regret having parted with this money. (*He puts the notes in his pocket.*)

SAM. No. It's a relief, I assure you.

VICAR. Yes—yes. Moth and rust, and so on. And depend upon it, my dear sir, you will be repaid an hundredfold.

SAM. Not in the same currency, I hope.

VICAR. Indeed no. In a less material currency, Mr. Jackson.

ALICE. (*Intervening.*) Now do come and sit down, Vicar.

JAMES. (*Moving Up Center.*) Yes, do sit down. (*He signals to* PAT *to return the watch.* PAT *nods.*)

ALICE. How is Mrs. Wedderburn?

VICAR. Mrs. Wedderburn?

ALICE. You left us a little while ago to go and call on her.

VICAR. (*Sitting on the sofa at the left end.*) Of course—so I did.

(SAM *sits in the armchair Down Left.* JAMES *sits in the armchair Left Center.* PAT *rises, crosses to the desk, surreptitiously affects to take the watch from the drawer and crosses to Right of* JAMES.)

ALICE. How did you find her?

VICAR. I'm afraid I didn't. I felt constrained to return here immediately.

PAT. (*Interposing.*) Have you lost something? Something you thought you might have left here?

VICAR. No, I don't think that's why I came.

PAT. (*Suddenly.*) Oh, Vicar, look at your coat. You've dropped ash all down it. Stand up and let me brush it off for you.

(PAT *assists the* VICAR *to rise, and brushes the front of his coat with her hand. As she does so, she exchanges a significant glance with* JAMES, *who smiles and nods with approval.*)

VICAR. Thank you, my dear. That's very kind of you. Now what was it I came back for? Ah, yes. (*He resumes his seat on the sofa.* PAT *moves above the sofa to the armchair Right Center and sits.*) I was crossing the road—not looking where I was going, I'm afraid—when all of a sudden it struck me.

ALICE. Good gracious! Not a car?

VICAR. Oh no. What actually struck me was—that I had left without congratulating you. That was what I came for, you know. You must be very pleased, Mr. Winter—very pleased.

JAMES. (*Bewildered.*) Oh yes—er—delighted.

VICAR. A very responsible position. But I'm sure your son is a reliable boy.

ALICE. Peter?

VICAR. I only found out by accident—quite by accident. I happened to go in, and I was having a word with the manager.

JAMES. The manager of what?

VICAR. The bank. The Inland Counties bank. The one your son has joined.

PAT. (*Rising.*) Peter in a bank?

VICAR. I'm sure he'll do very well. Such opportunities.

(SAM *sits up.*)

JAMES. Do you mean that my son has got a job in a bank?

VICAR. Surely you know?

JAMES. (*Rising; hurriedly.*) Oh yes, of course I know. I wasn't sure about the details.

VICAR. Oh, yes. The manager told me he had never seen such excellent testimonials. All of them from persons who had passed away, unfortunately, but most enthusiastic.

SAM. They would be.

(*The* VICAR *takes out his watch, looks at it in surprise, puts it to his ear, and listens with a delighted smile.*)

VICAR. (*In pleased surprise.*) Oh! It's going. When I was outside just now, I couldn't find it, and I came to the conclusion it must have stopped. (*He looks at his watch.*) Dear me, I had no idea it was so late. I must say good night. (*He rises.*) No, no, there is no need to see me out.

I have my umbrella. Good night. Good night, Mr. Jobson. Good night. (*The* VICAR *exits Up Center.* JAMES *follows him into the hall, waves farewell and returns immediately.*)

PAT. (*Sitting in the armchair Right Center.*) Peter in a bank!

ALICE. I told you he wouldn't let us down.

PAT. I mean, right in the bank.

ALICE. (*Complacently.*) Peter was always the one with brains. And you were losing faith in him.

SAM. (*Rising.*) Well, well—I must be getting back to my parish. Good night, Mrs. Winter. You're going to be proud of that son of yours. (*He moves above the sofa.*) We'll be hearing more of him.

JAMES. Not too much, I hope.

SAM. (*To* PAT.) Good night, little one.

PAT. Good night, sweet prince. (SAM, *to whom this quotation is unfamiliar, looks puzzled, then exits Up Center.* JAMES *follows him off. She rises, collects her bag and wrap and moves above the sofa.*) I must be off, too.

ALICE. Have a good evening, dear. I wouldn't say anything to Ronnie—about his father, I mean—if I were you.

PAT. As if I should.

ALICE. He may be sensitive, poor boy. And don't be too late.

PAT. I'll try not to be. Good night, Mother darling. (*She leans over the back of the sofa and kisses* ALICE, *then moves to the door Up Center.* JAMES *enters Up Center.*) Good night, Father.

JAMES. I hope you have a successful evening, my dear.

PAT. Same to you.

JAMES. Thank you very much. (*He moves to Left of the sofa.* PAT *exits Up Center. He smiles.*) I knew Peter must be up to something after all these weeks. (*He chuckles.*) I should like to see those testimonials. (*He crosses to the fireplace, swings open the picture above the mantelpiece and takes a little kit of burglar's tools from the cupboard behind it.*)

ALICE. Are you going out too, dear?

ACT I WHITE SHEEP OF THE FAMILY

JAMES. (*Moving to the door Up Left.*) A little call to make. Purely speculative. (*He opens the door, reaches inside and collects his hat, mackintosh and scarf.*)

ALICE. Put your scarf on, James. You mustn't catch cold.

JAMES. No—no. Of course I won't.

ALICE. I know what you are. So careless about your health.

JAMES. But very careful about everything else. (*He winds the scarf round his neck.*) That all right? Fussy old dear, aren't you?

ALICE. (*Rising and arranging the scarf.*) Shall you be late?

JAMES. (*Putting on his mackintosh.*) That depends on others. Don't sit up for me.

ALICE. I'll leave your Horlicks in the fender.

JAMES. Thank you.

ALICE. Look after yourself, darling. (*She kisses him.*)

JAMES. If I don't—read the morning papers. (*He kisses her, then moves to the door Up Center.*)

ALICE. (*Sitting on the sofa.*) Got your latchkey?

JAMES. Several! (JAMES *exits Up Center as—*)

THE CURTAIN FALLS

ACT TWO

Scene 1

SCENE: *The same. The following morning.*

When the CURTAIN *rises it is a bright sunny morning. The French windows are open and the table on the terrace is laid for breakfast.* PAT *is seated Left of the breakfast table. She wears a negligée and is reading "The Times."* JANET *enters the terrace from Left. She carries a tray with a pot of coffee and a jug of milk, which she places on the breakfast table.*

PAT. (*Looking up.*) Where's everybody, Janet?
JANET. (*Standing above the table.*) Mrs. Winter's down in the kitchen. Mr. Winter isn't up yet.
PAT. I expect he came in late.
JANET. He often does, doesn't he?
PAT. Did you hear me?
JANET. I heard a car. Two o'clock, wasn't it?
PAT. Nearer three.
JANET. Did you have a good evening at the Opera?
PAT. I'm not complaining. What was the film like?
JANET. (*Moving above the table to Right of it.*) Rotten.
PAT. Bad luck.
JANET. (*Grinning.*) I don't mind. (*She comes into the room and stands at the right end of the window.*) I'm not complaining either.
PAT. (*Looking sharply at* JANET.) What have you been up to?
JANET. (*Taking a gold cigarette case from her overall pocket.*) It was easy—it was really.
PAT. Show me.
JANET. (*Moving to* PAT *and showing her the case.*) It's gold.

ACT II WHITE SHEEP OF THE FAMILY

PAT. I told you not to try anything. You're not half good enough yet.

JANET. (*Crossing to Left of the sofa.*) He was asleep.

PAT. Who was?

JANET. The old gentleman next to me.

PAT. (*Rising and moving above the sofa.*) It doesn't matter if he was dead. You've got to have a lot more practice before you start on the public.

(ALICE *enters Up Center.*)

ALICE. 'Morning, darling.

PAT. Hello, Mother.

ALICE. Anything the matter?

PAT. Whatever do you think? Janet made a start last night.

ALICE. What? At the pictures? Well, everybody has to start somewhere. Show me, Janet.

JANET. (*Holding out the case.*) It's gold.

ALICE. (*Kindly.*) Very nice. How did you do it, dear?

JANET. He was asleep.

ALICE. (*Laughing.*) Oh dear. Never mind, it's a beginning.

PAT. It was very naughty of her. I told her not to.

ALICE. But if he was asleep, dear . . .

PAT. You mustn't encourage her, Mother. She's got to have a lot more practice first.

ALICE. If you say so, dear. (*She sighs.*) But I'm so tired of losing my brooches and bracelets, and then finding Janet's got them.

JANET. (*Moving down Center; plaintively.*) I've got to practise on somebody.

ALICE. (*Moving to Left of* JANET.) I'm not blaming you. Of course you've got to practise. But Pat's quite right. You're not good enough yet. I always know when you take things I'm wearing.

JANET. (*Feeling in her pocket.*) Did you know I'd got these? (*She holds up a pair of ear-rings.*)

ALICE. (*Surprised.*) Good gracious! My ear-rings.

When did you get those? (*She takes the ear-rings from* JANET.)

JANET. (*Grinning with pleasure.*) Last night.

PAT. What's that she's got?

ALICE. My ear-rings. (*To* JANET.) How did you do that?

JANET. When I put your wrap round you.

ALICE. (*Pleased.*) And I never felt a thing. You must admit that's good, Pat. (*She moves below the table Right Center and fixes her ear-rings to her ears.*)

PAT. (*Perching herself on the left arm of the sofa.*) Not bad. Janet's going to be very useful if she doesn't start too soon. But no more nonsense in cinemas, or anywhere else. I'll tell you when you can begin working.

JANET. (*Moving to* PAT.) I can go on practising, can't I?

PAT. Practise here as much as you like. (JANET *moves to the door Up Center.*) Oh, and I'll have my wrist-watch back before you go.

(ALICE *moves to the breakfast table and picks up her unopened letters.*)

JANET. (*Moving to* PAT; *disappointed.*) Oh! I thought you didn't know.

PAT. Of course I knew. Here's yours. (*She holds out* JANET'S *wrist-watch.*)

(JANET *looks at her own wrist in surprise, and then stares at* PAT.)

JANET. When did you get that?
PAT. Just after you got mine.

(JANET *and* PAT *exchange the watches.* ALICE *moves to the desk, sits at it, and opens her letters.*)

JANET. (*With real admiration.*) You are clever, you are really.

ACT II WHITE SHEEP OF THE FAMILY 43

PAT. I have to be.

JANET. Do you think I shall ever be as good as you?

PAT. Yes, if you don't do anything stupid, and get yourself put away first.

JANET. Fancy you getting my watch.

PAT. Just to show you how it ought to be done.

(JAMES *enters Up Center. He wears his dressing-gown.*)

JAMES. (*Moving to Left of the armchair Right Center.*) Good morning, good morning. Ah! The sort of morning that makes you feel glad to be free.

(JANET *moves above* JAMES *to Right of him.*)

PAT. Sleep well?

JAMES. Yes, thanks to a glass of Horlicks and a clear conscience. Did you *glean* anything from the Opera?

PAT. In snatches, darling.

JAMES. Nothing like a good brass section for distracting attention. Seems to stun them. Any letters, Janet? (JANET *picks up the unopened letters from the table Right Center and with her right hand gives them to* JAMES. *At the same moment she removes his cigarette case from his pocket with her left hand, then moves to the windows.*) Put it back!. (JANET *moves to Right of* JAMES *and replaces the case.*) Any coffee, Janet?

JANET. I've just brought it fresh. (JANET *goes on to the terrace and exits to Left.*)

ALICE. What do you think, James? Janet got my earrings last night and I never felt a thing.

JAMES. She's coming on, isn't she?

PAT. Yes, but for God's sake don't encourage her. (*She looks at her newspaper.*)

JAMES. (*Mildly.*) All right, dear, if you say so. (*He looks at his correspondence.*) Hallo, here's a reminder from Dr. Barnado. I must remember to send my subscription. Make me out a cheque when you've finished breakfast.

PAT. How much?

JAMES. Five guineas.

PAT. What about the Assistant Commissioner, and the Prisoners Aid Society?

JAMES. Did I promise a subscription—apart from the collection?

PAT. I think he'll expect one.

JAMES. Oh, well—it's a good cause. Or is it?

ALICE. How do you mean—or is it?

JAMES. People like that are an interfering lot, in a way, you know. The moment a man comes out of prison they try to make him give up the only job he knows—and go straight.

PAT. That doesn't matter. They always fail.

JAMES. Yes, there is that. I don't suppose five guineas will do any harm.

(JANET *enters the terrace from Left. She carries a rack of toast which she puts on the breakfast table.*)

JANET. Here's your toast, Mr. Winter. Will you have it outside?

JAMES. Yes, please.

PAT. (*Rising and crossing to the breakfast table.*) I'll do those cheques for you. (*She puts the newspaper on the table.*)

JAMES. Thank you.

(JANET *exits on the terrace to Left.*)

ALICE. Where did you get to last night, James?

JAMES. Eh? Oh, the American Embassy.

PAT. Father! You didn't? Any luck?

JAMES. No. Marshall Aid's cleared them out. (*He puts his letters on the table Center then crosses to the breakfast table and pours himself a cup of coffee.*)

ALICE. You haven't told me anything about your evening, dear.

PAT. (*Crossing to Left of* ALICE.) I got a very nice

ACT II WHITE SHEEP OF THE FAMILY 45

diamond brooch. It was rather amusing. A woman dropped it in the foyer—right in front of me—so I picked it up and gave it back to her. I could see it was a really good one. Then at the end of the show she saw me again, and she said, "Do you know, my dear, I'm afraid there must have been something wrong with the fastening of my clasp—I've lost it again."

(*They all laugh.* ALICE *rises.*)

JAMES. (*Picking up his cup of coffee and crossing to the fireplace.*) I've been thinking about Peter.

(ALICE *goes on to the terrace and exits to Left.* PAT *sits at the desk.*)

PAT. What's he up to, Father?
JAMES. Haven't the slightest idea. But I've been considering the possibilities. (*He puts his cup and saucer on the mantelpiece.*) They're simply endless. (*He moves Down Center.*) You see, the trouble with forged notes is uttering them—getting them into circulation. You have to pay people to do that, and there's always the risk of their not being honest. Well, now, all Peter has to do is to substitute forged notes for those piles of real notes lying about behind the counter, and the bank will put them into circulation for him.

(ALICE *enters the terrace from Left and crosses to the table Center. She carries a bunch of flowers in a piece of newspaper, and arranges the flowers in the vase on the table Center.*)

PAT. And he gets the real notes in exchange.
JAMES. Exactly.
PAT. That's an idea.
JAMES. (*Moving Up Right.*) I'll tell you a better one. What happens to all the soiled and torn notes which the banks collect and send back to wherever they send them?

ALICE. I expect they have them dry-cleaned, dear.
PAT. Hardly! I think they're pulped.
JAMES. But are they examined, that's the point. If they aren't, why not substitute forged notes for those? You'd have a lot of dirty notes on your hands, but they're legal tender. What is more, there'd be no evidence if the notes you substituted were destroyed or pulped, and no-one would be a penny the wiser. (*He crosses to the fireplace and picks up his coffee.*)
ALICE. Or the worse.
PAT. It sounds a bit complicated to me.

(PETER WINTER *enters the terrace from Left.*)

JAMES. I must have a talk with Peter about it.
PAT. (*Seeing* PETER.) In that case, now's your chance.
JAMES. Eh? (*He puts his cup and saucer on the mantelpiece.*)

(PETER *crosses to Right of the sofa. His manner is hesitant and nervous.*)

ALICE. (*Turning.*) Peter! Darling, how are you? How wonderful to see you. (*She embraces him.*)
PETER. Hallo, Mother.
JAMES. (*Crossing above the sofa to Left of* ALICE.) Hallo, Peter, my boy. This is splendid. Have you had breakfast?
PETER. Yes, thank you, Father.
ALICE. How are you? You look thin.
PETER. I'm all right, Mother.
ALICE. Are you getting enough to eat?
PETER. Yes, of course.
JAMES. I think you're looking very well. As a matter of fact, we were just talking about you.
PETER. Oh?
PAT. Hallo, Pete. (*She starts to fill in two cheques.*)
PETER. Hallo, Pat.

ACT II **WHITE SHEEP OF THE FAMILY** 47

ALICE. All the same, I think you ought to have told us where you're living. Where are you living?

PETER. I've got a flat.

ALICE. But who looks after you?

PETER. There's a woman comes in. Don't fuss, Mother. I'm perfectly all right.

JAMES. Of course he's all right. (*He takes* PETER *by the arm and leads him Down Right Center.*) Come here, my boy. I want to talk to you. We've heard your news—about the bank, I mean. The Vicar told us last night. Splendid!

PETER. (*Staring at* JAMES.) Did you say splendid?

JAMES. (*Crossing to the fireplace.*) A marvellous idea. I don't know what you're planning to pull off, of course.

(ALICE *finishes the flowers, crumples the newspaper, crosses and puts it in the waste-paper basket.*)

PETER. I'm not planning to pull anything off.

JAMES. Here are one or two suggestions for you. What happens to all the soiled notes the bank collects?

PETER. I don't know.

JAMES. You could find out, I suppose!

ALICE. (*Crossing above* PETER *to Left of him.*) James! I haven't seen Peter for six weeks, and you start talking business the moment he walks into the house. (*She puts her right arm through* PETER'S *left arm.*)

JAMES. (*Surprised.*) Why not?

ALICE. Because I haven't seen him for six weeks—that's why not. (*To* PETER.) Have you had any more colds?

(JAMES *picks up his cup and sips his coffee.*)

PETER. No.

ALICE. You didn't take your cough mixture with you.

PETER. I bought some.

ALICE. Good boy.

PAT. (*Rising and turning.*) Is anything up, Peter?

JAMES. Of course not. What should there be up? Have some coffee, Peter.

PETER. No, I—don't want any coffee.

PAT. (*Crossing to Right of* PETER.) There is something up. They're not on to you, are they?

PETER. Who?

PAT. The police?

PETER. No. Why should they be?

PAT. Then it's a girl, I suppose. Come on. If you're going to be such an egg as to get married, out with it.

PETER. (*Turning and moving Up Center; annoyed.*) You shut up!

ALICE. Peter! That's not a nice way to talk to your sister.

PETER. (*Moving Left of the sofa.*) Then tell her to lay off.

JAMES. Come, come, Peter. You mustn't quarrel the moment you come in, you know. It's only Pat's peculiar sense of humour.

PETER. (*Moving below the Right end of the sofa.*) It's not that.

JAMES. I think you've been very clever. Just one of those little touches of genius which . . .

PETER. (*Interrupting; nervous and embarrassed.*) I say, Father—you've got to know sometime or other . . .

JAMES. Know what?

PETER. In future—*I'm going straight.*

(*The* OTHERS *stare at* PETER *in amazement.*)

ALICE. (*Sinking into the armchair Right Center.*) Peter!

PAT. (*Under her breath.*) I knew it! (*She turns and moves above the table Right Center.*)

(*There is a silence.*)

JAMES. (*Solemnly.*) Do you realize what you've just said?

PETER. (*Sitting on the sofa at the Right end.*) Yes, Father.

JAMES. But—my dear boy—you can't mean it.

PETER. I do mean it.

JAMES. But why? What has happened? Why do you want to do this terrible thing?

PETER. That's just it. It isn't terrible. For the first time in my life I'm going to be honest.

JAMES. How can you be? Your whole life—your whole upbringing . . . Why, there isn't a man in the profession can turn out banknotes like yours. And as for signatures—Jim the Penman at his best never beat them.

PETER. All that's going to be forgotten.

PAT. (*Crossing to Right of the sofa.*) You're crazy! How can it be forgotten?

JAMES. All right, Pat. You'd better leave me to deal with this.

(PAT *sits on the stool above the Right end of the sofa.*)

PETER. I'm sorry, Father, but I've already dealt with it. You thought I'd joined the bank to rob it—well, I haven't. I've joined it to become a bank clerk and an honest citizen.

ALICE. (*Much distressed.*) Oh, Peter—the disgrace of it. (*She weeps into her handkerchief.*)

JAMES. (*Crossing to Left of* ALICE *and putting his hand on her shoulder.*) There! You see the effect on your mother.

PETER. I'm sorry, of course, but—I'm tired of being a crook, that's all.

PAT. (*Rising.*) You've turned yellow, you mean.

PETER. (*Hotly.*) I'm not yellow! You've no right to say that.

JAMES. Of course she hasn't. Please don't interfere, Pat. (PAT *turns, crosses to the window and gazes out. To* PETER.) You say you're tired of being what you call a crook?

PETER. I'm honestly sorry, Father. I know what it means to you.

JAMES. (*Crossing to Left.*) I wonder if you do? I am a crook—though I don't very much care for the word. I prefer to call myself an individualist. As such, I think I may claim to be at the very top of my profession. If I had been say, a civil servant, or an explorer, or even an author, I should undoubtedly have been knighted. But a burglar, however eminent, cannot expect public recognition. (*He moves Up Left Center.*) It would, in fact, be a handicap. But what he *can* have is the respect of his fellow workers. For four generations my family—your family, Peter—have been what you so lightly dismiss as crooks. (PAT *turns and listens.*) Your mother's grandfather—your great-grandfather—was the most expert forger of his day. On both sides your forebears have been looked up to by hundreds of skilled workers in the most exacting profession in the world. I am proud to have maintained that position. And you have helped, Peter. I have been very happy to see the way—the brilliant way in which you have carried on the family tradition. Our name is widely respected. There isn't an operator in England—in Europe even—who doesn't know it. And now you propose to drag it in the mud. For what? Why? Because of some foolish scruple about honesty. What is honesty?

PETER. Not stealing from people.

JAMES. (*Moving below the Left end of the sofa.*) Are they any worse off?

PETER. Of course they are.

JAMES. (*Kindly.*) My dear Peter. If I relieve a duchess of a family heirloom, what happens? She gets rid of something she has got tired of wearing, draws twice its value from the Insurance Company, pays her dressmaker, and goes to the South of France on the balance. She benefits, her dressmaker benefits, and I benefit. Who loses?

PETER. The Insurance Company.

JAMES. The Insurance Company can't lose—get that

into your head. (*He moves Down Left.*) It's a most philanthropic act to divert some of their surplus profits to an impecunious Duchess. (*He crosses to Left Center.*) Everything is on the side of the Insurance Companies— the law of the land, the police, public opinion—to say nothing of all the ingenious people who waste their time inventing burglarproof locks. Yet I win. And the Insurance Companies go on building bigger and uglier offices, and doubling their capital every ten years. Who loses?

(PAT *crosses to Right of the armchair Left Center.*)

ALICE. (*Rising and moving to Right of the sofa.*) There, Peter. Now that your father's explained it all, I'm sure you won't . . .

(PAT *moves above the armchair Left Center to the fireplace.*)

PETER. (*Rising.*) It's no use, Mother. Stealing's dishonest.

JAMES. So is selling what you haven't got, and buying what you couldn't pay for if you got it, on the Stock Exchange. (*He crosses to Right and turns.*) That's done every day, by respectable gentlemen who live in Surbiton. Would you be ashamed of me if I did that?

PETER. (*Crossing to Left.*) I'm not going to argue about it. I've got an honest job, and I'm going to stick to it.

JAMES. How did you get it?

PAT. Yes. How did you get it?

JAMES. (*Crossing to Right of* PETER.) The Bank manager was very impressed with your testimonials, wasn't he?

PETER. (*Quickly.*) Nobody can check up on those.

JAMES. So I understand.

PETER. All right. I forged them.

JAMES. Exactly.

PETER. I had to. (*He sits in the armchair Down Left.*)

But that's the last job of that sort I'm going to do. I'm going straight, I tell you.

ALICE. (*Desperately.*) But, Peter, have you thought what people will say?

PETER. I don't care what people will say. I'm not going to come here any more.

ALICE. Peter!

JAMES. Why not?

PETER. (*Rising; distressed.*) But—don't you see—how can I? If I'm in a bank, I can't very well spend my spare time in a house full of . . .

JAMES. Crooks? But, my dear Peter, who knows we're crooks? Ask the Vicar. I am a most respected churchwarden—and a J.P.

ALICE. And Pat does the flowers every third Sunday.

JAMES. You see, you come of a most respectable family.

ALICE. We've always been most particular.

JAMES. Your mother's quite right, Peter. You're letting the family down. (*He indicates the portrait over the mantelpiece.*) Look at your great-grandfather. Look at that face. A noble face—but just a crook, from your point of view.

PETER. (*Stubbornly.*) So he was.

JAMES. But a very widely respected gentleman. One of the greatest philanthropists of his day.

PETER. At someone else's expense.

JAMES. Aren't they all?

PAT. What are you going to live on, anyway?

JAMES. Yes.

PETER. My salary.

PAT. Ten pounds a week?

JAMES. (*Moving Up Center.*) Ugh! (*He paces above the sofa to Right.*)

PETER. Not as much as that, if you want to know.

(ALICE *sits on the sofa.*)

PAT. And you're going to live on that? You're crazy! Ha! Wait till the first time you're hard up.

PETER. (*Angrily.*) What do you mean?

PAT. You know. A nice little cheque will go through one of the accounts at your bank—with a signature that's every bit as good as genuine.

PETER. You've no right to suggest that.

PAT. I wasn't suggesting—I was prophesying. (*She crosses above the sofa and stands Up Right.*)

JAMES. Now, Peter. I'm not going to be the conventional heavy father, and tell you never to darken my doors again, just because you've turned honest.

PETER. I'm sorry, Father. You'd better face up to it, and cut me off with a shilling.

PAT. (*Sarcastically.*) Or a five-pound note—one of your own.

JAMES. But I am going to say this. Get this into your head. You're an artist—a genius. It's not a thing that's under your control. You can no more give it up than Keats could give up writing odes to nightingales or Grecian Urns. You've got to recognize it, Peter. Nature intended you for a great career—a lucrative career—and you can't get away from it.

PETER. It's no use, Father.

JAMES. (*Moving to the window.*) I'll have another cup of coffee. This is a blow, Peter—a bitter blow.

PETER. I'm sorry, Father. (*He turns his back to the room and faces the fireplace.*)

(JAMES *looks doubtfully at* PETER, *then sits Left of the breakfast table and puts his head in his hands. There is a silence.*)

ALICE. (*Presently.*) Come and sit here by me, Peter.

PETER. It's no use, Mother.

ALICE. Well, come and sit by me just the same. After all, I haven't seen you for six weeks. (PETER *crosses and sits Left of* ALICE *on the sofa.*) I'm afraid you've upset your father.

PETER. If he won't see reason, that's not my fault.

ALICE. And I don't know what we're going to say to

people when they ask after you—what you're doing and so on.

PETER. Tell them the truth.

ALICE. (*Shocked.*) Oh, we couldn't do that.

PETER. Why not?

ALICE. We were all so proud of you—everybody was. And now to have to tell them that you're in a bank. It's almost as bad as if you'd joined the police.

PETER. I nearly did.

ALICE. Oh, no, Peter. I couldn't have borne that. The disgrace is bad enough as it is. And think of Pat. It won't be very nice for her.

PAT. Never mind me, Mother. I can look after myself, if Peter can't.

PETER. (*Angrily.*) I can look after myself without your help.

PAT. (*Moving below the armchair Right Center.*) I wonder. (*Suddenly.*) Of course there's a girl at the back of this.

PETER. (*Aggressively.*) Well? What if there is?

ALICE. Oh, Peter. Not one of the *public?*

PETER. She's not a crook, if that's what you mean.

PAT. (*Quoting sarcastically.*) "She was poor, but she was honest . . ."

PETER. (*Rising and moving aggressively to Left of* PAT.) Look here, I've had enough of you.

(ALICE *rises and crosses to the fireplace.*)

JAMES. (*Rising and moving between* PAT *and* PETER.) Peter—Peter. Going straight doesn't seem to have improved your temper.

PAT. Love's young dream. It takes them that way sometimes.

PETER. (*Angrily.*) I've told you before . . .

JAMES. (*Soothingly.*) Children—children. (*To* PETER.) Hasn't your mother persuaded you to see reason?

PETER. No.

PAT. And she won't. There's a girl in it.

ACT II WHITE SHEEP OF THE FAMILY

PETER. (*Aggressively.*) Why not?

ALICE. (*Crossing to Left of* PETER.) But a member of the public, dear.

PETER. And another thing. She wants to come here and meet you all.

PAT. (*Laughing.*) That puts you in a bit of a spot.

JAMES. Why should it?

PAT. I thought Peter was never going to darken our doors again.

PETER. I'm not—after she's been.

JAMES. How are you going to explain that to her?

PETER. I don't know. But I'm going to bring her here this evening. And you've all got to be decent to her.

JAMES. My dear boy, what do you expect us to be?

PETER. I know you will, Father. And Mother. (*He crosses below* JAMES *to Left of* PAT.) But Pat's got to be decent too. No funny business like pinching her watch, or anything.

(JAMES *moves to Right of* ALICE.)

ALICE. I'm sure Pat will behave herself, dear.

PETER. I'm not.

PAT. She shall go away thinking what a sweet angel sister you've got.

PETER. No need to make it too hard for yourself.

JAMES. After all, why shouldn't she come? Would you like me to invite the Vicar as further evidence of respectability?

PETER. (*Awkwardly.*) No, I—I only want her to see that I have got a decent family, that's all.

JAMES. (*Affectionately.*) Of course you do. And she shall. Bring her to dinner, eh, Alice?

ALICE. Oh, yes—yes, of course. I hope she won't be too difficult to talk to.

PETER. Thanks awfully, Father. I'm sorry about the other thing, but—well, I couldn't help myself, really.

JAMES. Forget it.

PETER. (*To* ALICE.) About eight?

ALICE. Yes, dear.

JAMES. Make it seven-thirty, and we'll have a few drinks first—just to lubricate the atmosphere.

PETER. (*Moving to the window.*) Righto.

(ALICE *sits on the sofa at the Right end.*)

JAMES. (*Calling.*) Peter. Just before you go. (*He takes a five-pound note from his dressing-gown pocket and winks at* ALICE.) What do you think of this?

(PETER *turns, crosses to Right of* JAMES *and looks at the note.*)

PETER. Rotten! Who did it?

JAMES. Somebody Sam dug up. (*He takes another note from his pocket.*) Not as good as this, eh?

PETER. Not in the same . . . (*His face suddenly lights up.*) That's one of mine. It's damn good, isn't it? I say, look at the difference.

JAMES. It certainly shows that one up.

PETER. I'll say it does! Look at that lettering compared with this. Cramped, isn't it? I don't know why other people don't seem to be able to get that sweep on a line. It's not difficult.

JAMES. Ah, but you see, you happen to be a genius at it.

PETER. (*Enthusiastically.*) You haven't got to be too timid. I always . . . (*His face suddenly changes and he stares in consternation at the note.*) It wasn't fair to show me that.

(PETER *hands the notes to* JAMES, *then turns and exits quickly on the terrace to Left.*)

PAT. Very subtle, Papa.
JAMES. (*Chuckling.*) Not bad.
ALICE. James, you're wonderful.
JAMES. Oh, I wouldn't say that. (*He looks at the*

notes.) What about giving him these for a wedding present?

PAT. Serve him right. Your cheques are finished. Will you sign them? I say, Mother, he never even told us her name.

(JAMES *crosses to the desk, sits and signs the cheques.* PAT *moves to Left of the armchair Right Center.*)

ALICE. We didn't ask him, dear.

(JANET *enters Up Center.*)

JANET. (*Announcing primly.*) The Vicar, madam.

(*The* VICAR *enters Up Center.* JANET *exits Up Center.*)

VICAR. (*Moving Down Center.*) Ah! My dear people. I am so happy to find you here together. (*He looks around and beams at them.*) What an occasion—what a happy occasion. (*He shakes hands with* ALICE.)

PAT. Is it?

VICAR. (*Crossing to* PAT *and shaking hands with her.*) Of course—of course. (*He turns to* ALICE.) Only yesterday I was congratulating you on—er—something or other—and now this gladsome news regarding your son.

JAMES. (*Rising and crossing to Right of the* VICAR.) Did you say news?

VICAR. Yes, yes. Your son has been to see me—first thing this morning—about putting up the banns.

PAT. Did he bring the bride with him?

VICAR. I'm not quite sure. Yes, I think he did.

ALICE. Did he tell you her name?

VICAR. Yes, I took particular note of that. It was the name of a large railway station. (*He pauses.*) I have it—Preston. That was it. Preston.

ALICE. (*Rising.*) Preston! But that was the name of the Commissioner!

VICAR. How happy you must all feel. How very, very happy. (*He beams benignly.*)

(*The awful truth dawns on the* OTHERS, *and they look at one another with growing horror.* ALICE *sinks on to the sofa and* JAMES *sinks into the armchair Right Center, as—*)

THE CURTAIN FALLS

ACT TWO

SCENE 2

SCENE: *The same. The evening of the same day.*

When the CURTAIN *rises the stage is empty, the windows are closed, the window curtains are open and the lamps are lit.* JANET *enters Up Center. She carries a tray with four sherry glasses, which she places on the table Right Center. She then crosses to the cabinet Down Right, bends down and unlocks it. An idea then occurs to her, and she re-locks the cabinet, removes the key and places it on top of the cabinet. She rises, moves quickly to the door Up Center, listens, and then crosses to the fireplace. She places the small footstool in front of the fireplace, stands on it, swings back the picture and takes out the kit of burglar's tools, which she places on the sofa. She takes a skeleton key from the kit, crosses to the cabinet Down Right, where she inserts the key into the lock and opens the door that way. Looking very pleased with herself, she takes a full decanter of sherry out of the cabinet and places it on the tray on the table Right Center.*

ALICE. (*Off; calling.*) Do hurry, James. You'll be late, you know.

ACT II WHITE SHEEP OF THE FAMILY 59

JAMES. (*Off; calling.*) All right, my dear. Don't worry.

(JANET *hastily relocks the cabinet, replaces the skeleton key in the kit and puts it in the cupboard behind the picture. She closes the picture and replaces the footstool above the fireplace. As she does so,* ALICE *enters Up Center, moves to the table Center and looks in the cigarette box.*)

ALICE. How are things in the kitchen, Janet?

JANET. Oh, the cooking's all right, but I don't like the look of *him*. He looks *straight* to me.

ALICE. That's part of his professional make-up.

JANET. I see. Who is he? (*She crosses to Left of* ALICE.)

ALICE. He's called Handsome Harry. Apart from his superb mushroom omelettes, Handsome is one of the cleverest burglars in London. (*She crosses to the fireplace.*) He learned cooking so that he could work first-class hotels and restaurants. And working in a first-class hotel would accustom anyone to bare-faced robbery.

JANET. That was smart, wasn't it?

ALICE. He is smart. You could learn a lot from Handsome Harry. So you see, all this may be very useful to you.

JANET. Thank you, Mrs. Winter. You're very good to me.

ALICE. Well, we're doing all we can to give you a really good start in life. And now there's something you can do to help us.

JANET. Yes. Anything, Mrs. Winter.

ALICE. Well—Mr. Peter's bringing a young lady to dinner tonight, and she's not—that is, she's . . . (*She hesitates.*)

JANET. Do you mean she's one of the public?

ALICE. Yes, that's just what I do mean. She's not one of us. You understand?

JANET. Like the Vicar, I've got to be careful what I say.

ALICE. You won't say anything. That's what I wanted to warn you about. Just act like an ordinary housemaid.

JANET. Yes, Mrs. Winter. (*She crosses to the cabinet Down Right and picks up two sherry bottles.*) He's not going to marry her, is he? (*She moves below the table Right Center.*)

ALICE. I hope not.

JANET. What does he want to go and do a thing like that for?

ALICE. Haven't you ever been in love, Janet?

JANET. Only with Errol Flynn at present.

(PAT *enters Up Center.*)

PAT. All ready for the fray, Mother?

ALICE. (*Crossing and sitting on the sofa.*) I think so. That's all, Janet. Learn all you can.

JANET. I'm learning a lot.

(JANET *exits Up Center taking the empty bottles with her.* PAT *crosses to the cabinet Down Right and mixes a cocktail in the shaker.*)

PAT. Handsome Harry's an absolute wizard. You should see the entrée.

ALICE. I hope I shall.

PAT. If she thinks this is how we live, Peter's girl friend will want a jolly good reason for not coming to dinner once a week.

ALICE. That's the idea. Peter can't tell her why he wants to drop his respectable family, so the more she wants to come, the more likely they are to quarrel.

PAT. Poor old Peter.

ALICE. It's for his own good.

PAT. Yes, you're quite right. He wouldn't stick the bank for ten minutes, if it weren't for this girl.

ALICE. You don't think he really wants to go straight—for any other reason?

PAT. (*Scornfully.*) Did you see his face when Father

showed him that fiver? Peter may be a halfwit in some ways but he's an artist. What is there for him in a bank, except temptation? And girl or no girl, he'll fall inside three months, if he stays.

ALICE. I hope you're right, dear, for his sake. But the girl is a complication.

(JAMES *enters Up Center.*)

JAMES. (*Moving Down Center.*) All cleared for action?
PAT. You sound very nautical. What about splicing the mainbrace?
JAMES. Yes, I think we might. What do you say, Alice?
ALICE. Not for me, dear. I'll wait. You have one.
PAT. I've mixed a pretty rousing cocktail. (*She pours a drink from the shaker into a glass.*)
JAMES. What have you put in it?
PAT. (*Crossing to Right of* JAMES.) Everything except dynamite. (*She hands the drink to him.*) Try that.

(JAMES *cautiously sips the drink.*)

JAMES. I'll have sherry. (*He puts his glass on the table Right Center and pours himself a glass of sherry.*)

(PAT *picks up* JAMES's *cocktail, crosses to the cabinet Down Right, puts the glass on it, then pours a cocktail for herself.*)

ALICE. I hope you haven't made it too strong, dear.
PAT. Just a gentle tonic, Mother.
JAMES. I can see this party's going to go with a bang.
ALICE. (*With a note of anxiety.*) I do hope it is.
JAMES. (*Crossing above the sofa to Right of the armchair Left Center.*) Why shouldn't it?
ALICE. Well, dear—if this girl's really the daughter of the Assistant Commissioner . . .
JAMES. Nonsense! All we know is that the Vicar says her name's Preston. For all we know it may be Wolverhampton.

ALICE. But supposing the Vicar is right—just for once?

JAMES. Even if he is, there are thousands of Prestons in London. And what is there about us to arouse suspicion? Am I a churchwarden for nothing? Anyhow, she's not one of the family yet.

PAT. (*Picking up her drink and crossing to the armchair Right Center.*) Or likely to be. (*She sits.*)

JAMES. That depends on whether we manage to reclaim Peter. It's obvious that he's taken this unhappy course on account of this girl.

PAT. That's what I say—get him out of the bank, and back on his proper job, and the girl will fade away. But how do we get him out of the bank?

JAMES. I've been thinking about that. (*He crosses to the fireplace.*) In fact, I've got a plan.

PAT. Good for you!

JAMES. (*Putting his glass on the mantelpiece.*) We've got to bring Peter down to earth. (*He crosses to Left of* ALICE.) He's got to be made to realize that the straight and narrow path may look attractive, but it doesn't lead anywhere. What is there in it for him? A bank manager at fifty!

PAT. He's just sowing his tame oats—he'll come back.

JAMES. But I don't want him to feel that he's gone too far to come back. That the narrow path is too narrow to turn round in.

ALICE. Very nicely put, dear.

JAMES. Fortunately, Pat, you've never had any desire to go straight.

PAT. Few girls have.

JAMES. Peter's just young. Youth breaking out. That—and this girl—have made him temporarily unable to see things in their proper perspective.

ALICE. He used to be so happy forging in his little den. I've heard him singing at his work for hours.

JAMES. (*Crossing to the fireplace and picking up his drink.*) He'll be singing again. This is just a phase. I never went through it myself, but I was never romantic.

ALICE. (*Coyly.*) Oh, James—you *were*.

ACT II   WHITE SHEEP OF THE FAMILY

JAMES. (*Crossing to* ALICE *and holding her hand for a moment.*) In another way, perhaps. But I never took a romantic view of earning an honest living. We have simply got to cure Peter of this dangerous nonsense. (*He crosses to the fireplace and stands with his back to it.*)

ALICE. But how?

PAT. You can't go to the bank manager and tell him Peter's the best forger since Jim the Penman.

JAMES. No, but we can plant some evidence of the fact.

PAT. Something that will get Peter kicked out?

JAMES. No, no. Nothing so crude. Simply induce in Peter a state of mind in which he will resign of his own free will.

PAT. A pretty tough proposition.

ALICE. How are you going to do it, dear?

JAMES. It's quite simple. I'll get into his bank to-night . . .

PAT. You mean burgle it?

JAMES. I shall "effect an entrance." That won't be difficult. I shall take with me a lot of Peter's notes—pound notes and five-pound notes—and substitute those for the real articles.

ALICE. What will you do with the genuine notes?

JAMES. (*Laughing.*) I dare say you and Pat will find a use for them.

PAT. Peter will be furious.

JAMES. Of course he will. But what a position to find himself in. He'll recognize the forged notes at once, of course, but he won't be able to issue them: he won't have the money to replace them with real ones; and he dare not point out that they are forgeries, because no-one but he could spot them.

PAT. So what?

JAMES. He'll realize that the whole thing's too difficult, and turn it in. (*He puts his glass on the mantelpiece.*)

ALICE. (*Dubiously.*) It may sound all right, but Peter won't like it.

JAMES. It is for his own good!

ALICE. Oh, yes, of course it's for his own good.
JAMES. Then what does it matter whether he likes it or not?

(*The front doorbell rings.* PAT *rises.*)

ALICE. (*Rising.*) Oh dear, here they are. Oh dear! (*She crosses and stands below* JAMES.)
JAMES. Now remember, keep off thin ice.

(*They* ALL *stand, tense, waiting in silence for a few moments.*)

ALICE. I do hope this girl's Christian name isn't a railway station, too. Victoria or something.
JAMES. We all ought to be doing something natural. You be shaking the cocktails, Pat. (PAT *crosses to the cabinet Down Right. He indicates the armchair Left Center.*) You sit here, Alice, ready to rise with a welcoming smile. (ALICE *sits in the armchair Left Center. He picks up his glass from the mantelpiece.*) I'll stand here—holding my glass—thus.

(*There is a pause, then* JANET *enters Up Center.*)

JANET. (*Announcing.*) The Vicar, madam.

(*The* VICAR *enters Up Center.* ALICE *rises, and* PAT *and* JAMES *relax.* JANET *exits Up Center.*)

VICAR. Ah, good evening, Mrs. Winter. Good evening, Mr. Winter. (*To* PAT.) Good evening, my dear.
PAT. (*Crossing to the table Right Center.*) Good evening, Vicar. (*She pours a glass of sherry for the* VICAR.)
VICAR. (*Moving to Right of the sofa and looking anxiously around.*) I hope I'm not intruding?
JAMES. (*Heartily.*) Not at all. You're all the more welcome because we weren't expecting you. (*He puts his glass on the mantelpiece.*)

ALICE. Come and sit down, Vicar.

VICAR. No—no. I won't come in. I only looked in to—er . . .

PAT. Have some sherry, Vicar. (*She puts the drink in his hand.*)

VICAR. (*Taking the glass.*) No, thank you, my dear. Yes—I suddenly remembered it. The railway station, you know.

PAT. (*Moving to Right of the table Right Center.*) But you told us. Preston.

VICAR. (*Surprised.*) Preston? Oh no, not Preston. Oh, no, no.

ALICE. What?

PAT. You said it was Preston.

VICAR. (*Puzzled.*) *Preston?* Did I say Preston? (*He laughs.*) Oh, no, no, no. Surely I didn't say Preston?

JAMES. (*Crossing to Left of the* VICAR.) You did, you know.

VICAR. Strange. I remember mentioning Derby. Or was it Stoke?

PAT. You were quite definite about it.

VICAR. (*Moving to Left of* PAT; *vaguely.*) About Stoke?

PAT. No—Preston.

VICAR. (*Distressed.*) Oh dear, oh dear. My memory again.

JAMES. (*Moving to Left of the* VICAR.) If it wasn't Preston, what was it?

(ALICE *crosses to Left of* JAMES.)

VICAR. (*Blankly.*) What was what?

JAMES. The railway station.

VICAR. Oh, the railway station. (*He suddenly realizes what he has said.*) Why, am I going somewhere?

PAT. (*Gently.*) No, Vicar. The name of Peter's girl friend. The same as a railway station. You said you'd remembered it.

VICAR. Of course—of course. Stupid of me. You must

forgive me. Yes, I remembered it quite suddenly. That's why I've come.

JAMES. And it wasn't Preston?

VICAR. (*Laughing.*) Oh, no, no. I can't think where you got that idea from. No, it was . . . (*He hesitates and then smiles benignly.*) Do you know, all this talk about Preston and Nottingham and so on, has quite driven it out of my head. But I shall remember it in a moment. (*He sits in the armchair Right Center.*)

(ALICE *crosses to the fireplace.*)

PAT. Well, at any rate, it's not Preston.

VICAR. Oh no—not Preston.

JAMES. (*Crossing to Left; quietly.*) That's a relief, anyhow.

VICAR. Would it be somewhere on the Brighton line, do you think? Croydon perhaps?

PAT. Or Three Bridges?

VICAR. I don't think it was a double name. (*Confidently.*) But it will come back to it.

(*The front doorbell rings.*)

JAMES. Too late, I'm afraid.

VICAR. (*Vaguely distressed.*) Oh, is it? I'm so sorry.

ALICE. Never mind, Vicar. We shall soon know.

JAMES. Now, Pat—are we all ready? (*He picks up his glass from the mantelpiece and stands with his back to the fire.*)

(ALICE *sits in the armchair Left Center.* PAT *crosses to the cabinet Down Right and picks up the cocktail shaker. They wait and look expectantly at the door Up Center. The* VICAR *looks at them in surprise.*)

VICAR. (*Looking from one to the other; puzzled.*) Are you expecting somebody?

PAT. (*In a loud whisper.*) Our railway station.

ACT II WHITE SHEEP OF THE FAMILY 67

(JANET *enters Up Center.*)

JANET. (*Announcing.*) Mr. Peter, madam, and a lady.

(*The* VICAR *and* ALICE *rise.* ANGELA PRESTON *and* PETER *enter Up Center.* ANGELA *is a very pretty and self-possessed girl aged about twenty.* JANET *eyes* ANGELA *with interest and exits Up Center.*)

PETER. (*Leading* ANGELA *Up Left Center.*) This is Angela, Mother.
ALICE. (*Crossing to* ANGELA.) Angela! What a pretty name—like its owner.
ANGELA. (*Smiling.*) Thank you.
ALICE. (*Indicating* JAMES.) This is Peter's father.

(ANGELA *crosses to* JAMES. PETER *kisses* ALICE, *then crosses above the sofa to the* VICAR *and shakes hands with him.*)

JAMES. (*Shaking hands with* ANGELA.) How do you do, Angela? Isn't it an awful thing to find oneself suddenly surrounded by a gang of strangers?

(PETER *moves Down Center.*)

ANGELA. You don't make me feel like a stranger.
JAMES. That's very nicely put, my dear.
PETER. (*Relaxing.*) This is my kid sister, such as she is.

(ANGELA *crosses to Left of* PETER.)

PAT. (*Crossing to Right of* PETER; *brightly.*) No impertinence. (*To* ANGELA.) How do you do? (*She shakes hands with her across the front of* PETER.)
ANGELA. How do you do? I've seen you before.
PAT. Oh? Where?
ANGELA. At the Opera last night. It was during the interval. You were standing next to a woman smothered in diamonds.

PAT. (*Moving Down Right.*) Yes, I seem to remember her.

PETER. You know the Vicar, of course, dear.

ANGELA. (*Smiling.*) Of course.

VICAR. (*Shaking hands with* ANGELA.) Oh, have we met before? That's very nice. (*He pauses and thinks.*) Ah—of course! I hope you had a nice honeymoon.

PETER. That comes later, Vicar. We're not married yet.

VICAR. (*Concerned.*) Oh, aren't you? I say, I didn't forget the ceremony, did I?

PETER. No—and we'll see that you don't. Now, don't you think we might drink the bride's health?

JAMES. (*Crossing with his glass to the cabinet Down Right.*) A very good idea. (*To* ANGELA.) I warn you, the cocktails are mixed with dynamite.

(*The* VICAR *moves above the table Center, smells at the flowers on it, then turns and gazes out of the window.*)

PETER. Who mixed them?

PAT. I did.

PETER. (*To* ANGELA.) Have sherry. (*He turns to the table Right Center and pours a glass of sherry.*)

ANGELA. I think I'd like a cocktail.

(JAMES *pours two cocktails and hands them to* PAT.)

PAT. Good for you. Don't be bullied by a rat like Peter.

PETER. Who's a rat?

PAT. You are. Didn't you know? (*She hands a cocktail to* ANGELA.) Try this.

(ANGELA *takes the drink and sits in the armchair Right Center.*)

JAMES. (*Crossing to the table Right Center.*) Sherry for you, Peter?

PAT. (*Handing a cocktail to* PETER.) He'll have a cocktail or nothing.

(JAMES *pours out a glass of sherry.*)

PETER. All right. I'll take a chance.
JAMES. You've got one, haven't you, Vicar?
VICAR. (*Looking at his drink in surprise.*) Yes. Someone must have handed it to me.

(PETER *moves above the table Right Center, then below it.* JAMES *picks up the two sherries from the table Right Center and crosses with them to* ALICE.)

JAMES. (*To* ALICE.) You and I are too old to play about with high explosives. (*He hands her a drink.*) That's quite innocuous.
ALICE. Thank you, my dear.

(PAT *crosses to the cabinet Down Right for her own cocktail.*)

JAMES. Has everybody got a drink?
PAT. I think so.
JAMES. Now . . .
VICAR. (*Raising his glass; suddenly.*) To crime!

(*They* ALL *look at him in surprise.*)

JAMES. (*Startled.*) To crime?
VICAR. (*Smiling benignly.*) Oh—it's just an expression, you know. I can't remember where I heard it.
PAT. Probably from the Archdeacon.
JAMES. Never mind, Vicar. I'll give you a toast. A charming one. (*He raises his glass.*) To Angela.
PETER. (*Raising his glass.*) Angela.

(*The* OTHERS *echo the toast and they all drink.* ANGELA *smiles happily at them.*)

ANGELA. You're all very sweet.

JAMES. We're most happy to welcome you here, my dear.

ANGELA. You nearly didn't, you know.

JAMES. (*Crossing and perching himself on the Right arm of the sofa.*) Oh? Good gracious, how was that?

ANGELA. I had an awful job getting Peter to bring me. He didn't seem to want us to meet at all.

(*There are a few somewhat nervous laughs. The* VICAR *wanders above the sofa and the armchair Left Center to the fireplace and looks up at the portrait over the mantelpiece.*)

JAMES. Oh, nonsense!

ANGELA. I couldn't make out whether it was me he was ashamed of, or his family. (*She smiles.*) Now that I've met the family, I'm afraid it must be me.

PAT. (*Moving to the cabinet Down Right.*) We'll have another on that. (*She picks up the cocktail shaker, moves to* ANGELA *and* PETER *in turn and refills their glasses.*)

JAMES. We haven't dealt with this one yet.

PAT. We have. Same again?

PETER. Why not?

JAMES. (*To* ANGELA.) You must put down Peter's reluctance to bring you to the fact that he didn't want to share you with anyone else.

PETER. Can you blame me?

ALICE. (*Sitting on the sofa.*) It was very selfish of you, Peter.

PAT. (*To* ANGELA.) Did you like your cocktail?

ANGELA. Very much.

PAT. Good. Aren't you going to try one, Father?

JAMES. Not if I can possibly avoid it.

PAT. (*Replacing the shaker on the cabinet Down Right.*) The trouble with the older generation is that it can't drink.

JAMES. The trouble with the younger generation is that it can't stop.

ACT II WHITE SHEEP OF THE FAMILY 71

ANGELA. You'd get on very well with my father, Mr. Winter.

JAMES. (*Rising.*) Your father. Now—who is . . . ?

ANGELA. He says half the crime today is due to excessive drinking by the young.

VICAR. A very interesting theory. I was talking to a burglar only yesterday.

JAMES. A burglar?

VICAR. Yes. I visit at the prison, you know. Such cultivated people, some of them. Have you ever met any?

ANGELA. (*Rising.*) Well, as a matter of fact, I am rather interested . . . (*She crosses toward the* VICAR.)

ALICE. (*To* ANGELA; *quickly.*) Come and sit here, dear.

ANGELA. Thank you. (*She sits Left of* ALICE *on the sofa.*)

VICAR. This particular man was a cat . . .

JAMES. (*Crossing to the* VICAR; *quickly.*) Sit down, Vicar.

VICAR. (*Moving Down Left.*) Oh, no—I can't stay. (*He sits in the armchair Down Left.*) I only called in to—er—something to do with British Railways, I think. I shall remember presently.

JAMES. (*Moving and standing Left of* ANGELA.) We shall look forward to that.

ANGELA. (*Looking around.*) I love this room. (*She indicates the portrait over the mantelpiece.*) Whose portrait is that?

JAMES. My grandfather.

ANGELA. He's got a very benevolent face. There must be a lot behind it.

(PETER *moves above the table Center.*)

JAMES. There is.

(*The front doorbell rings.*)

PAT. That sounds like Sam Jackson.

(PETER *moves above the sofa and stands behind* JAMES'S *right shoulder.*)

PETER. (*Dismayed.*) Sam Jackson! (*To* JAMES. *Sotto voce.*) I say, Father, you can't . . . (*He hesitates.*)
JAMES. (*Moving to the fireplace.*) Why not?
PETER. (*Moving to* JAMES; *horrified.*) You didn't ask him?
JAMES. No, but I shall have to now, shan't I?
PETER. But, Father. . . . Just think . . .

(JANET *enters Up Center.*)

JANET. (*Announcing.*) Mr. Jackson, madam.

(SAM *enters Up Center.* JANET *exits.*)

SAM. (*Boisterously.*) Well, well, well, here we . . . (*He sees the* VICAR *and checks himself.*) Good evening, friends. Do I intrude?
JAMES. Not at all. Come in, Mr. Jackson.
SAM. (*Moving to Left of the sofa and shaking hands with* ALICE.) Good evening, Mrs. Winter. How are you, Reverend? (*To* PETER.) Well, my boy, this is great news I hear about you. Have you started in on the job yet? Or have you come to pick up a few tips from your Dad? If you have . . .
PETER. Started? (*He indicates* ANGELA.)
JAMES. (*Intervening.*) This is a purely social occasion. (*To* ANGELA.) My dear, let me introduce an old friend of the family—Mr. Jackson.

(SAM *shakes hands with* ANGELA. JAMES *crosses to the fireplace and presses the bell-push.*)

ANGELA. How do you do?
SAM. Very pleased to meet you. I haven't seen you here before, have I?
ANGELA. (*Smiling.*) No, actually, Peter brought me.

ACT II   WHITE SHEEP OF THE FAMILY   73

JAMES. In point of fact, these young people have just become engaged.

SAM. Engaged? Blimey O'Reilly! (*He corrects himself.*) My heartiest good wishes to you both. (*Jocularly.*) Trust young Peter to pick one out of the right stable. (PAT *moves to the cabinet Down Right and pours a drink for* SAM.) You're going to be one of us, I presume, my dear?

ANGELA. I hope so.

SAM. And what's your particular line?

ANGELA. (*Puzzled.*) Line?

SAM. Your line of country. Where do you operate? Inside or outside.

ANGELA. I'm afraid I just keep house for my father.

SAM. Your father, eh? I wonder if he's a client of mine, by my chance. What's his line?

(JANET *enters Up Center, moves to the windows and closes the curtains.*)

JAMES. (*Loudly.*) Pat. Give Mr. Jackson a drink. Jackson. A word in your ear. Come into my office. (*To* ANGELA.) Excuse us, please.

(JAMES *and* SAM *exit Left.* PETER *closes the door behind them.* PAT *crosses to the table Right Center and puts* SAM'S *drink on it.*)

ALICE. (*To* ANGELA; *resolutely changing the subject.*) What a pretty brooch you're wearing, my dear.

ANGELA. It is nice, isn't it?

ALICE. It looks most unusual. May I see?

ANGELA. Father brought it as a present from Switzerland. It's in two pieces. I'll show you.

(PAT *crosses to Right of the sofa to look at the brooch.*)

ALICE. Really?

ANGELA. The two sides come apart. (*She removes the*

brooch.) Then you can wear them as clips, like this. (*She demonstrates, fastening the clips on to her dress.*)

(JANET *crosses, stands above the Left end of the sofa and looks at the brooch.* ALICE *looks up and sees* JANET.)

JANET. (*Primly.*) Did you ring, madam?
ALICE. Yes. Mr. Jackson will stay to dinner, Janet.
JANET. Yes, madam.

(JANET *exits Up Center.*)

PAT. Let me see.
ALICE. Very ingenious.
PAT. (*To* PETER.) It's lovely. I must look out for one like it.
PETER. (*Moving to Left of* ANGELA; *with a warning look at* PAT.) I bet you half a crown you don't find one.
PAT. Done. I'll take it.
ANGELA. I won five shillings with it last night.
PAT. Oh! How?
ANGELA. I wore it to the Opera. Father didn't want me to, so I bet him twenty to five in shillings I wouldn't lose it.
ALICE. Why should you lose it?

(SAM *and* JAMES *enter Left.* JAMES *moves to the fireplace.* SAM *crosses above the sofa to the table Right Center and picks up his drink.*)

ANGELA. There have been a lot of cases of things being taken at the Opera lately—jewellery—bracelets and necklaces and things.
ALICE. Oh?
ANGELA. There were five plain-clothes men on duty at *Covent Garden* last night.
PAT. I only spotted four. (*She pulls herself up.*) Did they have any luck?

ACT II WHITE SHEEP OF THE FAMILY 75

ANGELA. I don't think so. I just sat there and watched them getting more and more bored.

PETER. (*Changing the subject.*) Talking about Opera . . .

VICAR. (*Rising.*) Opera! Dear me, it's time I left for Evensong. (*He puts his glass on the mantelpiece and crosses to* ALICE.)

ALICE. (*Rising and shaking hands with the* VICAR.) Good night, Vicar, and thank you for coming in to see us.

(ANGELA *rises.*)

VICAR. I always come at once when I have any special piece of news for you—in case I forget it, you know. Well, I have remembered it this time. (*He crosses to* SAM *and shakes hands with him.*) Good night, Mr. Derby. (*He turns and shakes hands with* PAT.) Good night, my dear. (*He moves to* ANGELA.) And good night to you, Mrs. . . . (*He gazes at her, evidently trying to recall her name.* JAMES, PAT *and* ALICE *all listen eagerly. He shakes hands with* ANGELA.) Good night. (PETER *moves to the door Up Center and opens it. He crosses to* PETER.) Good night, my boy. I have congratulated you on your new appointment, have I not?

PETER. Yes, thank you.

VICAR. Ah, what a career lies open to you. Keep on and on—forging ahead—forging ahead.

(*The* VICAR *exits Up Center.* JAMES *crosses and follows him off.* ANGELA *sits in the armchair Left Center.* PETER *closes the door and crosses to Right of* ANGELA. PAT *crosses and sits Down Left.* ALICE *resumes her seat on the sofa.*)

PAT. (*To* ANGELA.) Isn't he sweet?

ANGELA. I adore him. I loved the way he talked about crime and burglars. When there's a really good burglary in London, I always discuss it with Father.

SAM. (*Sitting in the armchair Right Center; interested.*) Is that his hobby? Crime stories?

(JAMES *enters Up Center.*)

ANGELA. (*Smiling.*) I don't know whether you could call it a hobby. Of course, most of the crimes are very simple—just breaking and entering, really.

JAMES. (*Perching himself on the Left arm of the sofa; smiling.*) What about all the unsolved ones?

ANGELA. They're not really unsolved. The police usually know all about them, but they can't make an arrest till they get the evidence.

SAM. But they've got to get it first, ain't they—h'm—have they not?

ANGELA. And they nearly always do, in the end. I think it would surprise a good many people who are living highly respected lives today, if they realized what a lot was known about them by the police.

JAMES. I sincerely hope the Winter family isn't under observation.

(ALICE *and* PAT *laugh lightly, followed by a guffaw from* SAM, *who quickly checks himself.*)

ANGELA. I must ask my father.

JAMES. I should like to ask him myself. I'm greatly looking forward to meeting him.

ALICE. We are all looking forward to meeting him.

ANGELA. I think you'll have a lot in common.

JAMES. I'm sure we shall. He seems to have a high opinion of the Police Force.

ANGELA. Well, he ought to. He says they know all the burglars in London.

SAM. (*With relief.*) Not all, they don't.

ANGELA. Oh?

JAMES. (*Hastily.*) I know what Mr. Jackson is thinking of. The burglary at the Duke of Troon's house.

ANGELA. (*Nodding.*) All the stuff was sent back by post.

JAMES. Oh, you know about that.

ANGELA. (*Smiling.*) Father has a theory about it.

JAMES. Has he? What is your father's theory?

ANGELA. He thinks the Duke did it himself.

JAMES. I know that dukes are often peculiar, but why should a duke burgle his own house?

PAT. For the insurance, of course. Dukes are so hard up nowadays they'll do anything for a spot of ready money.

ANGELA. No. Father said it was the publicity he was after.

PAT. Why should a duke want publicity?

JAMES. Anything to get tourists to visit their stately homes at a couple of bob a time.

ANGELA. But there was Mrs. Brainton-West as well.

PAT. What happened to her?

ANGELA. Her flat was burgled. Ten thousand pounds' worth of jewellery. That was sent back, too.

JAMES. And does your father think the Duke of Troon did that as well?

SAM. More likely Mr. Butler.

PAT. He wouldn't have sent it back.

ANGELA. Father's got another theory about that.

PETER. (*Determined to change the subject.*) I've got a theory about another drink. (*He crosses to the cabinet Down Right.*) What about you, Sam?

SAM. (*Rising and moving Down Right.*) I'm right behind you, my boy.

(PETER *pours drinks for* SAM *and himself.*)

ALICE. (*To* ANGELA; *conversationally.*) Where exactly do you live, dear?

ANGELA. In Westminster. One of those little streets just behind the abbey.

ALICE. Oh really. It must be nice to be able to pop into the Abbey whenever you want to.

ANGELA. I'm afraid I don't. We really live there because it's handy for Scotland Yard.
SAM. (*Turning and staring at* ANGELA.) Scotland Yard!

(JANET *enters Up Center.*)

JANET. The Commissioner again, madam.
ANGELA. (*Rising excitedly.*) My father! He said he'd come if he could—and here he is. (*Delightedly.*) Oh!

(ANGELA *runs to the door Up Center and exits.* SAM *chokes violently over his drink.* PAT, JAMES *and* ALICE *rise.* JANET *exits Up Center.*)

SAM. Blimey! A perishing copper!

(SAM *puts his glass on the table Right Center, moves quickly to the window, struggles with the curtains, opens the window and exits. The Winters survey one another with consternation.*)

ALICE. Oh dear. The name was Preston after all.
JAMES. (*Crossing above the sofa to Right of it; to* PETER.) Why didn't you tell us, my boy?
PETER. You never asked me.
JAMES. We never had the chance.

(ANGELA *and* PRESTON *enter Up Center.*)

ANGELA. Here he is.
PRESTON. (*Moving above the sofa to* ALICE.) May I intrude for a moment, Mrs. Winter? Uninvited as usual.
JAMES. (*Moving below the sofa.*) Yes, of course. Come in. This is a real surprise.
PRESTON. I've had a little surprise of my own.
JAMES. Oh?
PRESTON. Do you know, I had no idea, until this child

told me when she was coming this evening, that Peter was in any way related to you?

JAMES. We had no idea that Angela was related to you. No—no idea at all. Had we? (*To* ALICE *and* PAT.) Had we? No—no idea at all. But now that we're all going to be related to each other—you must stay to dinner.

PRESTON. With the greatest of pleasure.

JAMES. *Capital!* Capital! (*To* ALICE *and* PAT.) What?

CURTAIN

ACT THREE

SCENE: *The same. The following morning.*

When the CURTAIN *rises the french windows are open and the table on the terrace is laid for breakfast.* JANET *is standing Right of the breakfast table, removing the dirty china, but leaving one place set at the Left end. She is humming to herself. The telephone rings,* JANET *comes into the room, moves to the desk and lifts the receiver.*

JANET. (*Into the telephone.*) Primrose four-seven-three-two . . . Yes, miss. (*She recognizes the caller's voice.*) Oh, yes, Miss Preston . . . No, this is Janet, miss—the housemaid. (*She listens for a moment, registering apprehension.*) You say you lost something here last night, miss? . . . Oh! Yes, miss. It's been found. . . . In the—the dining-room, miss. You must have dropped it. . . . During dinner, I should think, miss. . . . Yes, it is fortunate, miss. . . . I'll tell her. Thank you, miss. (*She replaces the receiver.*)

(JAMES *enters Up Center and stands in the doorway. He wears his dressing-gown and a scarf.*)

JAMES. Good morning, Janet.

(JANET, *startled, turns and looks anxious.*)

JANET. Good morning, sir.
JAMES. (*Moving to the breakfast table.*) Any coffee?
JANET. I've just brought it fresh.
JAMES. Good.
JANET. Shall I make some more toast?
JAMES. (*Sitting at the Left end of the breakfast table.*) No. Just coffee, thank you.

ACT III WHITE SHEEP OF THE FAMILY

(ALICE *enters Up Center.*)

ALICE. Oh, there you are, Janet. (*She moves Left of the sofa then below it.*) I've been looking for you. Come here a minute, will you? (JANET *crosses to Right of* ALICE.) The brooch I was wearing last night, please. You took it during dinner.

JANET. (*Taking the brooch from her pocket and handing it to* ALICE.) I thought you didn't know.

ALICE. Know? You almost stabbed me to the heart. If I hadn't been sitting next to the Commissioner, I should have screamed.

JANET. Oh, madam, you'd never do a thing like that.

ALICE. I think you'd better stick to ear-rings when we have visitors, Janet.

JANET. Very good, madam.

(JANET *moves to the breakfast table, picks up her tray, then exits on the terrace to Left.* JAMES *picks up the newspaper from the table, rises and crosses above the sofa to Left of* ALICE.)

JAMES. (*Kissing* ALICE.) Good morning, my dear.

ALICE. Good morning, dear.

JAMES. None the worse for last night's festivities?

ALICE. No, I think it all went off very nicely, don't you? In fact, I thought the Commissioner would never go. Did you get into the bank all right, dear?

JAMES. (*Glancing through the newspaper.*) Yes.

ALICE. Were you successful?

JAMES. I was—and I wasn't.

ALICE. Now, James, is that all you're going to tell me?

JAMES. Yes, dear.

ALICE. Oh! (*She crosses to the desk.*) Well, I shall make out my weekly shopping list. (*She sits at the desk and makes notes.*) I wonder if he could get us a saddle of mutton.

JAMES. Who?

ALICE. Sam Jackson. He said he would be coming

found this morning; and he knows so many really obliging people in the black market.

(JAMES *crosses to the breakfast table and pours himself a cup of coffee.* PAT *enters Up Center.*)

PAT. Hallo, Mother. Busy?
ALICE. Just doing my shopping list, dear. Why?
PAT. It doesn't matter. (*She moves to* JAMES.) Good morning, Father. (*She kisses him.*)
JAMES. Good morning, my dear. You're very late. Were you working last night?
PAT. No. But I'm feeling slightly shattered this morning. Still, the party went off wonderfully well, considering.
JAMES. Yes. Congratulations to all concerned. Particularly you, Alice.
PAT. Hear! Hear! You made a real conquest of the Commissioner, Mother. What were you talking about?
ALICE. About eggs, dear. He can't get any either. I said I might be able to help him there.
JAMES. (*Laughing.*) Well, I must go and finish dressing, particularly if Sam's coming round. Always treat a fence with respect. (JAMES *crosses and exits Up Center.*)
PAT. (*Moving above the table Right Center.*) You know, I like that girl.
ALICE. (*Preoccupied.*) Yes, dear. What girl?
PAT. Your future daughter-in-law. You met her, if you remember, at dinner last night.
ALICE. I'm sorry, dear. I was thinking about something else.
PAT. (*Exasperated.*) Why does she have to be a policeman's daughter?
ALICE. (*Calmly.*) Only her mother could tell you that, dear.
PAT. Of course it just makes nonsense of the whole thing.
ALICE. What thing, dear?
PAT. Peter's romance—if it is a romance. He's far too good to waste his life in a bank. (*She sits in the arm-*

chair Right Center.) If she were the daughter of anything else—but a policeman! It's impossible.

ALICE. (*Still preoccupied.*) Oh no, dear. Lots of policemen have daughters.

PAT. Now, Mother. Stop talking like the Vicar. Do you think Peter's really serious about that girl?

ALICE. Oh yes, quite serious.

PAT. Isn't there anything we can do?

ALICE. Now, trust in your father, dear. He's got a plan. Do you remember, he told us so yesterday evening.

PAT. Did he go out last night, as he said he would?

ALICE. Yes.

PAT. What happened?

ALICE. I don't know yet. He's in one of his uncommunicative moods. (*She rises.*) Now I must see about lunch. Is there anything you want Sam Jackson to get for you?

PAT. I could do with some more nylons, as usual.

ALICE. (*Adding it to her shopping list.*) Nylons. I'll tell him. (JANET *enters Up Center. She carries an empty tray.*) All right, Janet, you can clear away the rest of the breakfast things. I don't think Mr. Winter will be wanting anything more.

JANET. Very good, madam. (ALICE *exits Up Center.* JANET *moves to the breakfast table, hesitates a moment, puts her tray on the table, then crosses to Left of* PAT. *Nervously apprehensive.*) The young lady who was here last night rang up.

PAT. Oh! What about?

JANET. (*Anxiously looking at* PAT.) I meant to put it back, I did really, but I didn't have a chance.

PAT. So it's like that, is it? Come on. What have you got? (JANET *apprehensively takes one half of* ANGELA'S *brooch from her pocket.*) Now you have done it. You know she's Peter's girl friend, I suppose?

JANET. Yes.

PAT. And did you know her father's a policeman?

JANET. (*Frightened.*) I meant to put it back. I did really. I was only practising.

PAT. I've told you before, practise on the family, not on visitors. What did you tell her when she rang up?

JANET. I said it had been found.

PAT. It would serve you right if she came for it and brought her father with her.

JANET. (*Frightened.*) She won't do that, will she?

PAT. Don't be a little idiot. Why should she? Where did you say it had been found?

JANET. In the dining-room.

PAT. All right. (*She takes the brooch.*) I'll see she gets it back.

JANET. Oh, thank you.

PAT. And don't do it again.

JANET. I won't. Really, I won't.

(*The telephone rings.* PAT *rises, crosses to the desk and lifts the telephone receiver.* JANET *crosses to the breakfast table and commences to stack the tray with the breakfast things.*)

PAT. (*Into the telephone.*) Hallo. . . . Yes, it's me speaking. . . . How are you, Auntie? . . . What? . . . Have you? That's very sweet of you. Yes, of course I'll come. . . . Now? . . . No, I'm not doing a thing. . . . Yes, I'll come right away. Good-bye. (*She replaces the receiver.* JAMES *enters Up Center and crosses to the fireplace. He is now fully dressed. She moves to the door Up Center.*) That was Aunt Susan. She picked some rings up somewhere last night, and she wants me to go round and choose one for my birthday. (PAT *exits Up Center.*)

JAMES. (*Taking a cigarette from the box on the mantelpiece.*) Half a minute, Janet. I'd like some more coffee. (*He lights his cigarette.*)

JANET. Righto, Mr. Winter. (*She glances off Right.*) Oh, here's Mr. Jackson.

JAMES. Where?

JANET. Coming up the garden.

(JANET *picks up the laden tray and exits on the terrace*

to Left. SAM, *whistling cheerfully, enters the terrace from Right. He puts his hat on the breakfast table, and comes into the room.*)

JAMES. Hallo, Sam. How are you?

SAM. (*Crossing to Right of* JAMES.) Not too bad. That copper didn't 'arf give me a turn last night. I only just got away in time.

JAMES. You missed a very good dinner.

SAM. Well, did you go along to the bank last night, like you said you were going to?

JAMES. Yes.

SAM. All O.K.?

JAMES. I got in easily enough.

SAM. I'm sure you did. What happened then?

JAMES. I found it had been burgled.

SAM. Burgled! What were the police doing, for goodness sake?

JAMES. Disgraceful, wasn't it? Somebody had been there before me. And a very nice job it was, too. Not a lock broken. The combination on the safe hadn't been forced. Just opened.

SAM. (*Laughing.*) Ah! I get you. Of course. (*He sits in the armchair Left Center.*)

JAMES. What do you mean—of course?

SAM. Well, Peter hasn't stuck to the straight and narrow very long, has he?

JAMES. You think it was Peter?

SAM. Of course it was Peter. Who else could it be? To open a safe like that you must know the combination.

JAMES. Not always. There have been men who could do it by a kind of instinct. It depends how sensitive your fingers are. You can sort of feel the tumblers moving.

SAM. Only a very rare bird can do that. Could you?

JAMES. I have done it, but I can't do it every time.

SAM. (*Confidently.*) It was Peter all right, you can bet your boots on that.

JAMES. It couldn't have been. He's not such a fool. He'd be the first person to be suspected.

SAM. The money was gone, I suppose?
JAMES. Not a banknote left in the place.
SAM. (*Rising.*) Well, how could you think it was anybody else but Peter?
JAMES. Because Peter isn't a burglar. He's only a forger. Burgling's not his line at all. He hasn't got the talent. (*He shows* SAM *a small object concealed in the palm of his hand.*) Besides, whoever did the job, dropped that by the door of the strong-room. And it wasn't Peter.
SAM. Well, what did you do?
JAMES. I left the forged notes as arranged, and came away. After all, it doesn't matter who actually got away with the real notes, so long as we planted Peter's stuff for him to find. All the same, I'd like to know who did it.

(JANET *enters Up Center. She carries a small tray of coffee for two.*)

JANET. (*Putting the tray on the table Center.*) Here's your coffee, Mr. Winter.
JAMES. (*Crossing to the table Center.*) Thank you, Janet. Bring another cup, will you? Peter's coming.
JANET. Oh, I didn't know he was coming.
SAM. Are you expecting him?
JAMES. Aren't you?

(JANET *exits Up Center.*)

SAM. (*Nodding.*) Yes. Now you mention it, I am. If he was the burglar, of course he'll come. And if he wasn't the burglar, well, he'll come just the same. (*He sits in the armchair Left Center.*)
JAMES. (*Pouring coffee.*) Yes. But who did the job, Sam? I'll swear there's nobody we know who could have opened that combination. (*He picks up a cup of coffee and the sugar basin and crosses to* SAM.)
SAM. (*Taking six lumps of sugar one at a time and putting them in the coffee.*) I couldn't agree with you more, old man.

ACT III WHITE SHEEP OF THE FAMILY 87

JAMES. Can't you give a guess? You know everybody in the profession.

SAM. Perhaps it was one of them interfering crooks from the Continong.

JAMES. No, no. He wouldn't bother with a little bank like that. Sugar?

SAM. (*Putting two more lumps of sugar in his cup.*) Ta. (*He shrugs his shoulders.*) I dunno. I give up. (JAMES *moves to the table Center and collects his own cup of coffee.*) Perhaps we'd better call in the Assistant Commissioner.

(*They* BOTH *laugh.* JANET *enters Up Center. She carries a tray with a cup, saucer and spoon.*)

JAMES. Thank you, Janet. (*He takes the tray and puts it on the table Center.* JANET *exits Up Center. He moves to Left of the sofa.*) Now, the only thing to do is to wait for Peter.

SAM. You won't have to wait very long.

JAMES. No. The bank'll be open by now.

SAM. What sort of line's Peter going to take about this? He's in a bit of a spot, you know.

JAMES. He'll have no choice. (*He sits on the sofa.*) He'll have to leave the forged notes and resign his job, while the going's good.

SAM. Oh well, we can only wait and see.

JAMES. Yes.

(*They* BOTH *sip their coffee in silence. After a few moments* PETER *enters Up Center and moves between* JAMES *and* SAM. *Neither takes any notice of him. He looks at them both, then crosses below the sofa to Right of it and throws his hat onto the stool Right of the sofa.*)

PETER. What's the big idea, Father?

(JAMES *rises, moves above the sofa and puts his cup on the table Center.*)

JAMES. (*Feigning surprise.*) Peter! My dear boy, delighted to see you. Have some coffee?

PETER. I don't want any coffee.

JAMES. Janet's brought a cup for you.

PETER. Oh, so you were expecting me.

JAMES. Of course. Sure you won't have some coffee?

PETER. Quite sure.

JAMES. Coffee braces the system.

PETER. Never mind my system. What's the meaning of all this? (*He takes a bundle of five-pound notes and some packets of one-pound notes from his pocket and tosses them on to the table Center.*)

JAMES. (*Perturbed; with a complete change of tone.*) Peter—you haven't done anything stupid, I hope?

PETER. I haven't. But I wouldn't answer for you.

JAMES. Aren't those some of the notes I left in the bank last night?

PETER. So it *was* you.

JAMES. Of course it was me.

PETER. I might have known it. Nobody else could have cracked the bank as neatly as that.

JAMES. Thank you, Peter.

PETER. (*Moving Right.*) Why did you do it? It was just damn silly.

JAMES. Never mind why I did it. You seem to have got yourself in a bit of a jam, my boy. You've brought those notes away from the bank and left nothing in place of them.

PETER. I've left the real notes in place of them.

JAMES. But the real notes weren't there.

PETER. (*Crossing to Right of* JAMES.) No, but fortunately I found them where you'd left them—in a neat parcel behind the bank door, addressed to me. If that was your idea of a joke, Father, it was a pretty poor one.

SAM. (*Rising.*) What!

JAMES. (*Incredulously.*) In a parcel—addressed to you?

PETER. You know perfectly well they were.

ACT III WHITE SHEEP OF THE FAMILY

JAMES. I know nothing of the kind. I didn't burgle the bank.

PETER. Come off it, Father. How did that money get there?

JAMES. I got into the bank—but I didn't burgle it. I didn't have to. The door was open.

PETER. How could it be open?

JAMES. Not only the door, but the safe—the strong-room—everything. And they were open because someone had been there before me.

PETER. Do you mean someone burgled the bank before you got there?

JAMES. Yes.

PETER. (*Incredulously.*) And are you suggesting it was they who left the money on the doorstep?

JAMES. Nobody else could have done it.

PETER. (*Crossing to Right.*) I'm sorry, Father, but you don't really expect me to believe that, do you?

(SAM *puts his cup on the mantelpiece.*)

JAMES. But, my dear boy, it's the truth.

PETER. The whole place was locked up when I got there this morning—the safe and everything.

JAMES. (*Moving below the sofa.*) Yes, I locked it.

PETER. (*Incredulously.*) You found the safe open and you locked it?

JAMES. Yes.

PETER. But there wasn't a lock damaged.

JAMES. No.

PETER. (*Crossing to Right of* JAMES.) Do you mean to tell me there's anyone in the country, except you, who could do a job like that, without damaging the locks—any of them?

JAMES. I know it doesn't sound possible, but whoever burgled that bank is an expert—as good as I am—probably better.

PETER. (*Moving Right Center.*) No, I—I don't mind admitting that when I saw how neatly the job had been done, and realized that you'd done it, I couldn't help feeling—well, a little bit proud of you, Father. That's why I'm not going to believe now that someone else did it. I've always known that you're the best cracksman of this generation, and I'm going to go on knowing it, whatever you say.

JAMES. (*Sitting on the sofa.*) No, Peter. I'm afraid I've got to admit a rival.

PETER. Are you really serious, Father?

JAMES. Really serious.

PETER. Then whoever it was who did that job, I'd like to meet him.

JAMES. So would I.

(PETER *is lost in admiration for a while, then he catches* JAMES'S *eye.*)

PETER. (*Moving to the door Up Center.*) I must get back to work.

SAM. Oh! So you're not going to resign from the bank?

PETER. (*Moving to Left of the sofa.*) No. And I've no intention of resigning. If that was your scheme, it was a flop.

JAMES. (*Rising.*) Peter, my dear boy. I'm older than you are. (PETER *crosses below* JAMES *and the sofa to Right Center.*) I admit that my little plan last night didn't work quite as I intended. But won't you please listen to reason?

PETER. It's no use, Father.

JAMES. I've known young men go straight before. From decent criminal families, too. (*He crosses to Left of* PETER.) And I've known them live to regret it. Fortunately, you've done nothing yet of which any of us need be ashamed.

PETER. No. And I'm not going to.

JAMES. But you won't be able to help it if you go on like this. Come back, Peter, and we'll forget the whole thing. I promise you nobody will ever hold it against you that you tried to go straight.

ACT III WHITE SHEEP OF THE FAMILY

PETER. I know you mean well, Father. But I've gone too far now to turn back, even if I wanted to.

JAMES. Not if you come back in the right spirit.

PETER. Good-bye, Father. (*He moves to the door Up Center and turns.*) Give my love to Mother. And tell Pat she's not such a bad sport, will you? (PETER *exits Up Center.*)

SAM. Not much of a success that little plan of yours.

JAMES. No. What do we do now? We can't just leave Peter to ruin his whole life.

SAM. (*Crossing to Left of* JAMES.) Why did someone have to burgle that bank the same night? And why leave the money on the doorstep? And who was the burglar? It's crazy!

JAMES. It's obvious. The man who burgled the Duke of Troon's house; the man who robbed the flat in Park Lane.

SAM. You don't go burgling in your sleep, do you, by any chance?

JAMES. Very much the reverse. Any other theory?

SAM. (*Shaking his head.*) I'm snookered, guv'nor.

JAMES. Think of something, Sam. (*He sits in the armchair Right Center.*) I'm very worried about Peter.

(PAT *enters Up Center.*)

SAM. Oh, you don't have to worry. He'll get tired of going straight in the end. They always do. Well, so long. I'll get along to the little back room. I don't like funny business. (*To* PAT.) Good morning, Princess.

(SAM *exits by the terrace to Right.* JAMES *takes from his pocket the article which he showed to* SAM *and carefully looks at it. After a few moments, he slips it back into his pocket.*)

PAT. Are you busy, Father?

JAMES. What? No, I was just a little preoccupied. Do you want something? Oh, did you get your ring?

PAT. (*Moving to Left of* JAMES *and holding out her hand.*) Yes.

JAMES. (*Glancing at the ring on* PAT'S *finger.*) It's a pity your Aunt Susan doesn't operate more frequently.

PAT. Was Peter here just now?

JAMES. Yes. He left a few minutes ago.

PAT. Oh! I wanted to see him, to give him this. (*She gives* JAMES ANGELA'S *clip.*)

(JAMES *takes the clip, glances casually at it, and then suddenly becomes interested.*)

JAMES. Where did you get this?

PAT. Well, actually that little idiot Janet got it last night from Peter's girl friend.

JAMES. Oh, she *did?*

PAT. Practising! I wanted to give it to Peter to give back to her. She rang up about it. Wanted to know if she'd lost it here.

JAMES. (*Amused.*) And she had?

PAT. Yes. Thanks to Janet.

JAMES. (*Intently examining the clip.*) Pretty, isn't it?

PAT. That's only half of it.

JAMES. So I imagine.

PAT. The two pieces clip together to make a brooch.

JAMES. (*Rising and crossing to the fireplace.*) Yes. I'll keep it. I'll give it to Peter when I see him.

PAT. What did you think of her?

JAMES. (*Preoccupied.*) Who? Angela? Oh, charming.

PAT. (*Perching herself on the Right arm of the sofa.*) I liked her. It's a pity about her and Peter. Of course the whole idea's impossible.

JAMES. Oh, I don't know. I have an idea everything may come right.

PAT. What makes you say that? Had a brainwave?

JAMES. No. Just a smile from fortune.

PAT. I must go and change in a minute.

JAMES. Going out?

PAT. Yes. When Mother comes back she wants me to

ACT III WHITE SHEEP OF THE FAMILY 93

go and have a look at Jameson and Carters—that big jewellers, you know.

JAMES. I know the establishment well.

PAT. You're not thinking of working it, are you?

JAMES. No. Jewellers' shops aren't worth my while. I prefer to wait until their contents pass into the hands of people who don't take the same precautions.

PAT. (*Rising.*) Oh well, I must be off. (*She sees the forged notes on the table Center.*) What's all this?

JAMES. Some of the stuff I left at the bank last night. Peter brought it back.

PAT. Brought it back? Then the plan didn't work, after all.

JAMES. It's a little complicated. If I could explain, I would. You might put it away somewhere, will you, please? If someone came in, it might look a little ostentatious.

(JAMES *exits Left.* PAT *begins to gather the notes together, stooping to look at some of them. As she does so,* JANET *shows* ANGELA *in Up Center.*)

JANET. I think he's in here, miss.

ANGELA. Oh, thank you.

JANET. (*Seeing* PAT.) Oh, I thought Mr. Winter was here.

PAT. (*To* ANGELA.) Hallo.

ANGELA. Hallo.

PAT. I know what you've come for. The clip you lost here last night.

(JANET *smiles broadly as* PAT *points the line for her.*)

ANGELA. (*Moving to Left of the table Center.*) Yes. Your maid said it had been found.

PAT. Yes. She found it.

ANGELA. (*To* JANET.) Thank you very much.

JANET. It was a pleasure, Miss.

PAT. Thank you, Janet.

(JANET *grins and exits Up Center.*)

ANGELA. I couldn't think where I'd lost it.
PAT. They come off very easily.
ANGELA. Yes. (*She indicates the notes.*) What's all this?
PAT. (*Calmly.*) I'm afraid my father's terribly careless about money. (*She collects up the balance of the notes.*)
ANGELA. It's rather a lot to leave lying about.

(PAT *crosses to the desk and casually puts the notes in the desk drawer.* ANGELA *watches her with rather puzzled interest.*)

PAT. It is rather. But it's just like Father. He's an absent-minded old dear. By the way, he's got your clasp. He was going to give it to Peter to give back to you.
ANGELA. I like your father.
PAT. (*Moving below the table Right Center.*) So do I. Cigarette?
ANGELA. (*Moving Down Right Center.*) No thanks, not now. I did enjoy the party last night.
PAT. Did Peter?
ANGELA. (*Sitting on the sofa; a little worried.*) I think so. But I'm a bit bothered about something he said to me on the way home.
PAT. (*Sitting in the armchair Right Center.*) Oh? What did he say?
ANGELA. He said—we shouldn't be coming here any more.
PAT. Did he give any reason?
ANGELA. No. Is there a reason?
PAT. Peter should know.
ANGELA. Do you?
PAT. I know what Peter's reason is. But it's up to him to tell you, not me.
ANGELA. Has he had a quarrel with his father or anything?
PAT. Good Lord, no. They adore each other.

ACT III WHITE SHEEP OF THE FAMILY 95

ANGELA. Perhaps your father doesn't like his being in the bank?

PAT. No. Not much.

ANGELA. Neither do I.

PAT. (*Surprised.*) You don't? Why not?

ANGELA. It's a dull job. Just routine. I don't think he likes it much, either. (*She rises.*) He hasn't always been in a bank, has he?

PAT. Er—no.

ANGELA. What was he before? (*She crosses to Left of* PAT.) But perhaps you'd rather I asked him?

PAT. (*Rising.*) I'd rather he answered. Look, I don't want all this to seem like a mystery, but—well, there are things . . .

ANGELA. That's why I'm here. I hate mysteries. Peter wouldn't give me any reason, so I've come to ask your father.

PAT. Supposing you don't get an answer to your mystery?

ANGELA. I'll find out the answer.

PAT. I doubt it.

ANGELA. So there is a mystery.

PAT. I didn't say so.

ANGELA. You're saying so all the time. If there weren't, you'd tell me why Peter doesn't want to come here any more. But I must know, if I'm going to marry him, mustn't I?

PAT. (*Desperately.*) Look, I'm not competent to deal with this. (JAMES *enters Left. She sees* JAMES.) Oh, thank God!

JAMES. (*Crossing to Left of* ANGELA.) Good morning, Angela.

ANGELA. (*Shaking hands with* JAMES.) Good morning.

JAMES. I was half expecting you.

PAT. (*With a rush.*) Father's got your clasp. He'll give it back to you. Do you mind if I go—I've got to change. (PAT *exits hurriedly Up Center.*)

JAMES. (*With a friendly smile.*) Would you like some coffee?

ANGELA. No, thank you.

JAMES. I always like people to like coffee, because then I can have some, you see. But it doesn't matter. (*He gives her the clip.*) Oh, your clasp.

ANGELA. Oh, thank you. But that's only half of it.

JAMES. Is it? I'm afraid that's all they found here.

ANGELA. Oh! I must have lost the other half somewhere else.

JAMES. What a pity. I suppose one half is no good without the other half.

ANGELA. Not much. But thank you for finding it.

JAMES. Not at all. Was that what you came for?

ANGELA. No—not really.

JAMES. I thought not.

ANGELA. It's rather difficult to . . .

JAMES. My dear, nothing's difficult when people are friendly with one another. (*He takes her by the hand and leads her to the sofa.*) Sit down. (ANGELA *sits on the sofa, at the Right end. He sits Left of* ANGELA.) Now tell me all about it.

ANGELA. Why are you so nice to me?

JAMES. Is there any reason why I shouldn't be?

ANGELA. You were all nice to me—last night. Mrs. Winter, and Pat, and you.

JAMES. Of course. After all, we're fond of Peter, and he brought you here.

ANGELA. You didn't—resent his bringing me?

JAMES. Actually I think we were all very relieved.

ANGELA. Why?

JAMES. Well, parents are naturally a little anxious when their son brings home the girl he wants to marry. We couldn't help comparing you with what he might have brought.

ANGELA. You mean you liked me?

JAMES. Oh yes. Very much.

ANGELA. Then why did Peter say we shouldn't be coming here any more?

JAMES. Didn't you ask him why?

ANGELA. He wouldn't tell me.

ACT III WHITE SHEEP OF THE FAMILY   97

JAMES. Oh!
ANGELA. I've just asked Pat, and she wouldn't tell me either.
JAMES. Oh!
ANGELA. Do you want to stop Peter from marrying me?
JAMES. On the contrary. I think you would make a most admirable wife for him.
ANGELA. (*Completely bewildered.*) Then what is it?
JAMES. Where did Peter tell you all this last night? At the bank?
ANGELA. No. On the way home from here. We didn't go to the bank. Why should we?
JAMES. No, of course not. It would be all shut up. What am I talking about? And he said he wouldn't be bringing you here any more?
ANGELA. Yes.
JAMES. Weren't you surprised?
ANGELA. Of course.
JAMES. Yes. Poor Peter. It must have sounded a little odd.
ANGELA. But why did he say it?
JAMES. I'm afraid he couldn't help himself.
ANGELA. Won't you please tell me? If I'm going to marry Peter, I've got to know, haven't I? What is the reason? Please.

(JAMES *looks at her and smiles in the friendliest way.*)

JAMES. Before I answer that question, my dear, do you mind if I ask you one first? It will make things so much easier.
ANGELA. No. Of course not.
JAMES. (*Kindly.*) Thank you. Why did you send back the Duke of Troon's heirlooms?
ANGELA. (*Rising; startled.*) I?
JAMES. (*Kindly.*) And the Park Lane diamonds?
ANGELA. (*Moving Right Center.*) What do you mean?
JAMES. (*Rising and crossing to Left of her.*) No, don't

go away, my dear. Sit down here. (*He leads her to the armchair Right Center.*) Sit down, please. You did send them back, didn't you?

ANGELA. (*After a pause.*) Why do you think . . . ?

JAMES. Last night, Peter's bank was burgled, and he found the money, in a parcel on the doorstep. Obviously the job had been done by the same person who effected an entrance—that's the proper term, you know—effected an entrance into the Duke of Troon's house, and so on.

ANGELA. (*Recovering.*) What have I got to do with it?

JAMES. (*Very matter-of-fact.*) It was you who burgled the bank.

ANGELA. Why should you think that?

JAMES. (*Handing her the other clip.*) That's the missing half of your clasp, isn't it?

ANGELA. Yes.

JAMES. You dropped it near the door of the strong-room. (ANGELA *droops in her chair.*) Most unfortunate, wasn't it?

ANGELA. (*Sharply.*) Who found it? Not Peter?

JAMES. Oh, no—no. Peter doesn't know that you were responsible. Oh no. It was you, of course?

ANGELA. (*After a moment's pause; reluctantly.*) Yes.

JAMES. Yes. And the Duke of Troon, and the rest of them?

ANGELA. Yes.

JAMES. Yes. Still you haven't answered my question yet, have you? Why did you send them back?

ANGELA. (*Rising, moving Right and standing with her back to him.*) What else could I do with them? I suppose you've finished with me now?

JAMES. (*Very sympathetically.*) Ohhh! Why should you suppose that?

ANGELA. I'm a criminal—a common burglar.

JAMES. Common burglars don't return the swag to the victims. (*He chuckles.*) In fact, I don't know any burglars who do. (*He moves Up Right and turns.*) Nor could any common burglar have got into that bank without

ACT III WHITE SHEEP OF THE FAMILY 99

breaking a single lock. (*He moves to Right of her.*) How did you do it?

ANGELA. (*Turning and facing Down Left.*) It was quite easy. Why do you want to know? (*She turns to face him.*) Why did you say I should make a good wife for Peter? You knew then I was a burglar.

JAMES. What made you begin burgling?

ANGELA. (*Moving Down Center.*) It was just fun, that's all. Ever since I can remember I've had burglar's tools to play with—probably the best collection in the country. (*She moves to Left of* JAMES.) I could unlock any door in our house before I was ten, without the key.

JAMES. Why did you unlock the Duke of Troon's door?

ANGELA. That was different. Father was always saying burglars were all stupid—

JAMES. Oh!

ANGELA. —how they all gave themselves away, and so on. So I did it to show him.

JAMES. But you didn't tell him?

ANGELA. No. I meant to. But afterwards—well, I didn't know how he'd take it. After all, it's his job, and he mightn't have liked being fooled by his own daughter.

JAMES. No—no. (*He laughs.*) The official mind. No breadth of vision.

ANGELA. (*Defiantly.*) Well? Do you still think I'd make a good wife for Peter?

JAMES. Tell me one thing. Are you sorry for what you've done?

(ANGELA *looks at him for a moment, then drops her head.*)

ANGELA. Yes.

JAMES. Truly sorry?

ANGELA. Yes. (*She pauses, then moves Left Center. Suddenly she raises her head, turns and looks defiantly at him.*) No, I'm not. I'm not sorry. I'd do it again. It was the most wonderful thrill I've ever had.

JAMES. Of course it was. (*Softly.*) Of course it was.

When you feel the skeleton key turn smoothly in the lock, and you push the door open—ever so slowly—and you stand there in the darkness—listening. Then you switch on your torch—do you use a torch?

ANGELA. (*Staring at him as though hypnotized.*) Sometimes.

JAMES. (*Softly.*) You switch on your torch—a little pool of light at your feet—and you move—step by step— (*He advances on* ANGELA. ANGELA *retreats.*)—slowly then swiftly to the foot of the stairs. You switch off your light—and stand listening—five minutes—ten minutes—listening to all the little night sounds which mean that the house is peacefully asleep. (*In a whisper.*) Only you are awake—alert—on the job. Then upstairs, to the first-floor bedroom—you open the door and slip in—somebody stirs in his sleep. You step back, motionless in the shadows—then silence. You move over to the dressing-table. That's where the stuff is. You're just about to lay your hands on it . . .

ANGELA. (*Sharply.*) How do you know?

JAMES. How do I know what?

ANGELA. How do you know what it's like? (JAMES *looks at* ANGELA *for a moment, then smiles broadly, crosses to the fireplace, swings open the picture and takes out the kit of tools.*) Oh! (JAMES *crosses to the table Right Center, puts the kit on it and opens it. She moves to Right of the table Right Center.*) Oh! Where did you get these from?

JAMES. You know what they are?

ANGELA. Of course. How did you get them?

JAMES. Nice, aren't they?

ANGELA. (*Picking up one of the tools and examining it.*) Marvellous!

JAMES. (*Handing her a skeleton key.*) Look at this key.

ANGELA. I've never seen one like that before.

JAMES. I invented it.

ANGELA. That would open anything.

JAMES. Practically. (*He hands her another tool.*) That's useful too.

ANGELA. What's it for?

JAMES. Sometimes a lock will stick half-way. Then you have to lift . . .

ANGELA. (*Eagerly.*) I know. You use it like that. (*She demonstrates.*)

JAMES. That's right.

ANGELA. (*Picking up another article from the kit.*) What's this for?

JAMES. Put it against the combination of a safe and you can hear the wards moving.

ANGELA. You don't need to hear them.

JAMES. It helps.

ANGELA. I can always sort of *feel* them moving.

JAMES. Not everybody can do that.

(ANGELA *picks up a jemmy. Suddenly she stares and drops it.*)

ANGELA. (*Backing Down Right.*) But—why have you got all these things?

JAMES. (*Quite calmly and casually.*) Because I use them. You see, I'm a burglar.

ANGELA. (*Staring in amazement.*) You're a—what?

JAMES. (*Calmly.*) A burglar—though I prefer to call myself a self-employed individualist.

ANGELA. Does Peter know?

JAMES. Of course Peter knows. That's why he said he wasn't bringing you here any more. He thought your father being a high-up in Scotland Yard, the two families wouldn't mix. (*He chuckles.*) I see his point.

ANGELA. (*Staring at him in bewilderment.*) And you were in the bank last night?

JAMES. Not very long after you.

ANGELA. But why were you there at all?

JAMES. A little plan to reclaim Peter. But you rather spoilt it.

ANGELA. How do you mean—reclaim him?

JAMES. Get him out of the bank. You see it's not . . . I'm afraid you're going to find this a little hard to understand.

ANGELA. Is Peter a burglar too?

JAMES. Oh, no, no, no. He's . . . (*He takes a five-pound note from his pocket, and hands it to her.*) Look, do you know what that is?

ANGELA. Yes. It's a five-pound note.

JAMES. Do you think it's all right?

ANGELA. Yes. Isn't it?

JAMES. No. It's a forgery. A very good one, of course.

ANGELA. How do you know?

JAMES. Because I know who made it.

ANGELA. Not—Peter?

JAMES. Yes. Peter's the cleverest forger in London.

ANGELA. No!

(JAMES *takes the note from her and holds it up to the light.*)

JAMES. You see that water-mark? You know it's always been the water-mark which has defeated people. The banks rely on it. Well, Peter has invented a way of putting the water-mark into the paper after the paper has been made. Nobody's ever been able to do that before. Now you see why we want to get him out of the bank.

ANGELA. (*Taking the note from* JAMES; *bewildered.*) But—isn't he in the bank on purpose?

JAMES. Well—it's not the kind of thing one likes to say about one's son—but as you're going to marry him, you'll have to know. (*He sadly shakes his head.*) He went into the bank to go straight.

ANGELA. (*Incredulously.*) You mean Peter was going straight for my sake? When he could do work like this?

JAMES. Yes.

ANGELA. (*Crossing to the sofa and sitting.*) The darling! Bless him!

JAMES. Angela! Do you care for him as much as all that?

ANGELA. (*Sincerely*.) I adore him.

JAMES. Then answer me one more question.

ANGELA. (*Happily*.) Anything you like.

JAMES. What was your motive? That's what I can't understand. Why, with all London to choose from, did you select Peter's bank to burgle?

ANGELA. (*Hesitating rather shyly*.) Well—I suppose it was horribly sentimental of me, but I simply couldn't resist the idea. This was going to be my very last job before I married Peter. After all, you can't have a bank-clerk with a burglar for a bride.

JAMES. Only an amateur burglar.

ANGELA. I'm as good as a professional.

JAMES. Yes—better than most. (*He moves below the table Right Center*.) Oh, I can assure you, we've followed your career with the greatest possible interest. The Troon heirlooms—the Park Lane diamonds—and so on. We've often discussed it amongst ourselves. (*He packs up the kit of tools*.)

ANGELA. Who?

JAMES. (*Crossing to the fireplace*.) Well, we're not exactly a trade union—just a bunch of burglars who get together on Wednesday nights to talk shop. (*He replaces the kit behind the picture and closes it*.)

ANGELA. I wish I could have heard you. Though I expect as a professional, you despised my methods.

JAMES. On the contrary.

ANGELA. Are you very good?

JAMES. (*Moving to the bookshelves*.) Good? Wait! (*He swings open the bookshelves, takes out the book of cuttings and hands it to* ANGELA.) My press notices. I'm not mentioned by name, of course—that's where the acting profession has an advantage—but I can always be relied on to make the front page.

(ANGELA *opens the book*.)

ANGELA. (*Eagerly*.) The Dartmoor diamonds—was that you?

JAMES. Yes. But I'm afraid they rather over-estimated the value of them.

ANGELA. And the Rajah of Waranapatan. Did you do that?

JAMES. (*Perching himself on the Left arm of the sofa.*) Ah, now they were real.

ANGELA. (*Turning a page.*) Not the Emery Street Safe Deposit?

JAMES. Money for jam!

ANGELA. What made you choose such a difficult one?

JAMES. Handy for the Tube.

ANGELA. Father had a theory it was the work of a Continental gang. He went to Paris to look for them.

JAMES. (*Rising.*) I know. I was very flattered. (*He crosses to Right.*)

ANGELA. Wasn't there a special burglar-proof combination lock on the safe?

JAMES. (*Moving to Right of the sofa.*) There certainly was. It took me twenty minutes to open it.

ANGELA. I've never met one I couldn't open right away.

JAMES. I'd like to see you open a safe.

ANGELA. I'd love to show you.

JAMES. (*Moving to* ANGELA *and taking her by the hand.*) You would? (ANGELA *rises. He takes the book from her and leads her to the safe Right.*) Step this way, will you? (*He indicates the panel.*) Help yourself.

(ANGELA *kneels, opens the panel and commences to work on the combination lock of the safe.*)

ANGELA. This is going to be easy.

JAMES. Haha! Don't you be too sure. I spent a lot of money installing that . . .

ANGELA. Sssssh!

JAMES. Sorry. (*He moves to the table Center and puts the book on it.* PETER *enters the terrace from Right and stands in the window. He motions* PETER *to silence.*) Sssssh!

ACT III WHITE SHEEP OF THE FAMILY

PETER. Sorry. (*He comes softly into the room and sees* ANGELA.)

(ANGELA *succeeds in opening the safe, and rises.*)

ANGELA. There you are.
PETER. What on earth . . . ?
ANGELA. (*Happily.*) Oh! (*She crosses to Right of* PETER.)
PETER. What are you doing here?
ANGELA. Oh, Peter. Were you really going straight for my sake?
PETER. (*Bewildered.*) Yes. (*To* JAMES.) What have you been telling her?
JAMES. (*Moving Up Left Center.*) The truth, Peter—simply the truth.
PETER. Look here. That's a bit too thick. You haven't told her . . .
ANGELA. Everything. And I think your notes are marvellous.

(PETER, *utterly bewildered, looks from one to the other. As he does so,* PAT *enters Up Center, and stands listening just inside the door.*)

PETER. You mean—you don't mind?
JAMES. (*Crossing to Left of* PETER.) Peter, meet the cleverest little amateur in the business. The Troon heirlooms—the Park Lane diamonds . . .
PETER. Am I crazy, or are you?

(PAT *moves Down Left Center.*)

ANGELA. Darling!
PETER. (*To* ANGELA.) You mean you did those jobs?
ANGELA. Yes.
JAMES. Congratulations, Peter. I always hoped we'd have another burglar in the family. What about the bank now, eh?

PETER. To hell with the bank! (*He embraces* ANGELA.)

JAMES. This is a truly moving moment. You don't know how happy you make me, Peter. This calls for a celebration. (*He crosses to the cabinet Down Right and pours sherry for five.*)

PAT. (*To* ANGELA.) I knew you were all right, the moment I saw you.

ANGELA. (*Crossing to* PAT.) Pat! (*She embraces her.*)

(*Unknown to* ANGELA, PAT *removes the bracelet from* ANGELA'S *wrist.*)

JAMES. But what brought you back, Peter?

PETER. (*Crossing to Left of* JAMES.) The Vicar turned up at the bank with five phoney notes to pay into his missionary fund. Where did he get them?

JAMES. (*Laughing.*) You know the Vicar. He would have them.

PETER. I came to have a row about it, but now—well, I suppose it's a bit different. (*He moves Center. To* ANGELA.) Were you really opening that safe?

JAMES. And a very nice job too. Fifteen seconds.

ANGELA. That's nothing. You should see me with a real safe.

PETER. (*Cheerfully.*) I say—this does make a difference, doesn't it? Did you really think my notes were good?

ANGELA. Marvellous. I want to know how you do them.

PETER. So you shall. I never realized till this minute how much I missed them.

ANGELA. (*Looking round at the* OTHERS.) But it's all too marvellous. (*To* JAMES.) You a burglar, and Peter a forger. (*To* PAT.) Where do you come in?

PAT. (*Smiling.*) Did you have a bracelet on when you arrived?

ANGELA. Yes. (*She looks at her wrist.*) Where is it? (PAT *holds out the bracelet.*) When did you get that?

(Peter *crosses to* Pat, *takes the bracelet from her and replaces it on* Angela's *wrist.*)

Pat. A moment ago.
Angela. You mean, you're . . . ?
James. Pat has the cleverest fingers in the country.
Angela. (*Realizing.*) The Opera! That's why you were there.
Pat. The intervals are most useful.

(Alice *enters the terrace from Right and comes into the room. She wears outdoor clothes.*)

Alice. Hallo, Peter, my dear.
Peter. (*Crossing to* Alice *and embracing her.*) Hallo, Mother, I must tell you all about Angela. She's . . .
Alice. I know, dear. I overheard it all. I was listening.
Angela. (*Crossing to* Alice *and embracing her.*) Oh, Mrs. Winter—isn't it wonderful? (*Suddenly.*) Oh, what a lovely brooch!
Alice. Yes, it is nice, isn't it? I picked it up whilst I was out.
Angela. (*Realizing.*) Picked it up! What a family!

(James *crosses with his tray of sherries and hands them round. During the following speech* Alice *sits in the armchair Right Center*, Angela *and* Peter *sit side by side on the sofa, and* Pat *perches herself on the Right arm of the armchair Left Center.*)

James. And thanks to you, my dear, once more a united family. Our white sheep is back in the fold, none the worse for his lapse into virtue, and together we can now continue to make our modest, but not inconsiderable contribution to national recovery. (*He puts the empty tray on the table Right Center, then stands below the Right end of the sofa.*) Money will be more plentiful in the country, thanks to Peter, and the luxury trades will be busier than ever, as a result of our activities. Our family is united, our consciences are clear, and our future is assured. This would be a happier and a better country if everyone could say as much. (*He raises his glass.*) I give you—Private Enterprise.

ALL. Private Enterprise. (*They* ALL *rise and drink as—*)

THE CURTAIN FALLS

THE WHITE SHEEP OF THE FAMILY

FURNITURE AND PROPERTY LIST

ACT ONE

On Stage:

Cabinet (Down Right). *On it:* silver tray with ¼-full whisky decanter, ½-full sherry decanter, 2 empty sherry bottles, bottles of gin, French vermouth, Italian vermouth, bitters, whisky, 3 whisky glasses, 4 sherry glasses, syphon of soda, ½-full cocktail shaker, napkin.

Key in cabinet lock.

In it: 1 full decanter of sherry, 4 cocktail glasses.

Writing desk with drawer. *On it:* blotting pad, stationery, pens, pencil, inkstand, cheque-book, lamp, telephone, vase of flowers, magazine.

Desk stool.

Waste-paper basket.

Safe in wall behind concealing panel. *In it:* cigar box of jewellery with smaller box inside it containing diamond necklace.

Table (Right Center). *On it:* table lighter, large ashtray concealing gold watch, silver box of cigarettes.

Armchair (Right Center).

Sofa. *On it:* 3 cushions—centre one without cover, 3 cushion covers, needle threaded with cotton.

Table (Center). *On it:* vase of flowers, work-basket containing scissors, matches, silver box of cigarettes, ashtray.

Stool (Center).

Stool (below sofa). *On it:* silver ashtray, matches in silver holder.

Pedestal stand (Up Center). *On it:* lamp.

Table (Up Left Center). *On it:* lamp, box of cigars.

Bookshelves. *In them:* books.

FURNITURE AND PROPERTY LIST

In cupboard behind right section: news-cutting book, pot of paste and brush.

Armchair (Left Center). *In it:* cushion without cover.

Occasional table (Left Center). *On it:* ashtray, matches.

On mantelpiece: clock, mirror, ornaments, box with cigarettes, ashtray, matches.

Over mantelpiece: hinged portrait of elderly Victorian gentleman.

In cupboard behind picture: kit of burglar's tools, containing torch, skeleton key, lock lifter, listening gadget, jemmy.

Armchair (Down Left). *On it:* cushion without cover.

Stool (above fireplace).

Pictures on walls.

2 pairs of electric-candle wall-brackets.

Light switches Left of door Up Center.

Bell-push by fireplace.

Carpet on floor.

Pair of window curtains and pelmet.

Small pair window curtains and pelmet.

In hall: chair, table, pictures.

On terrace: breakfast table.

3 chairs.

Fender.

Hearthrug.

Fire screen.

Off Stage:

Large silver tray. *On it:* silver coffee-pot with coffee, stand with spirit burner, silver bowl with sugar, jug with milk, 5 each coffee-cups, saucers, spoons (JANET).

Visiting card (JANET).

Evening Standard, Evening News, and *Star* (JAMES).

Hat, mackintosh, scarf (JAMES).

Personal:

JAMES: coins.

PAT: bracelet, bag, wrap.

SAM: wad of one-pound notes, six one-pound notes, one

five-pound note, jeweller's glass, carnation, cigarette case, lighter.
VICAR: gold watch, hat.
ALICE: cigarette case, lighter.
PRESTON: lighter.

ACT TWO

SCENE 1

Strike:

Occasional table Left Center.
Stool below sofa.
Sherry decanter and all sherry glasses.
Work-basket and flowers from table Center.
Remains of newspaper.
One-pound notes from desk.
Dirty coffee-cups.

Set:

On breakfast table: tablecloth, 3 napkins, bowl of fruit, 3 knives, 2 small plates with toast remains, 2 each coffee-cups, saucers and spoons. At Left end: clean plate, knife, 2 each coffee-cups, saucers and spoons, dish of marmalade, dish of butter, copy of *The Times*, 5 letters for ALICE, wrist-watch for PAT.

On table Right Center: 5 letters.

On table Center: empty flower vase.

Off Stage:

Tray. *On it:* pot of coffee, jug of milk (JANET).
Rack of toast (JANET).
Roses in newspaper (ALICE).

Personal:

JANET: gold cigarette cases, wrist-watch, ALICE's earrings.
JAMES: cigarette case in right-hand pocket, five five-pound notes.
ALICE: handkerchief.

Scene 2

Strike:

Breakfast things from breakfast table.
Cup and saucer from mantelpiece.
Cheque forms and five-pound note from desk.

Set:

Decanter of sherry in cabinet.
4 cocktail glasses on cabinet Down Right.
3 whisky glasses on cocktail cabinet Down Right.

Replace:

In cupboard behind picture: kit of burglar's tools.

Off Stage:

Tray with 4 sherry glasses (JANET).

Personal:

ALICE: brooch.
ANGELA: 2-piece brooch.

ACT THREE

Strike:

Dirty glasses.

Set:

Breakfast table as for Act Two, Scene 1.
On cabinet Down Right: tray with 6 sherry glasses.

Off Stage:

Tray (JANET).
Tray. *On it:* jug with coffee, jug with milk, sugar bowl with lump sugar, 2 each coffee-cups, saucers and spoons (JANET).
Tray. *On it:* coffee-cup, saucer and spoon (JANET).

Personal:

JANET: ALICE'S brooch, half of ANGELA'S brooch.
JAMES: 2 five-pound notes, half of ANGELA'S brooch.
PETER: packet of five-pound notes, packets of one-pound notes.
ANGELA: bracelet.
PAT: ring.
ALICE: brooch.

www.ingramcontent.com/pod-product-compliance
Lightning Source LLC
Chambersburg PA
CBHW072014290426
44109CB00018B/2231